# The Vortex

# Other Hay House Titles by Esther and Jerry Hicks

(The Teachings of Abraham®)

## Books, Calendar, and Card Decks

*The Law of Attraction* (also available in Spanish)

*The Amazing Power of Deliberate Intent* (also available in Spanish)

*Ask and It Is Given* (also available in Spanish)

*Ask and It Is Given Cards*

*Ask and It Is Given Perpetual Flip Calendar*

*The Astonishing Power of Emotions* (also available in Spanish)

*The Law of Attraction Cards*

*Health, and the Law of Attraction Cards* (available April 2010)

*Manifest Your Desires*

*Money, and the Law of Attraction* (book; CD program; card deck)

*Sara, Book 1: Sara Learns the Secret about the Law of Attraction*

*Sara, Book 2: Solomon's Fine Featherless Friends*

*Sara, Book 3: A Talking Owl Is Worth a Thousand Words!*

*Spirituality, and the Law of Attraction* (book; CD program— both available January 2011)

*The Teachings of Abraham Well-Being Cards*

## Additional CD Programs

*The Teachings of Abraham Master Course Audio* (11-CD set)

*The Law of Attraction* (4-CD set)

*The Law of Attraction Directly from Source* (1 CD)

*The Law of Attraction in Action* (2-DVD set)

*The Amazing Power of Deliberate Intent* (Parts I and II: two 4-CD sets)

*Ask and It Is Given* (Parts I and II: two 4-CD sets)

*The Astonishing Power of Emotions* (8-CD set)

*Sara, Books 1, 2, 3* (unabridged audio books; 3-CD sets)

## DVD Programs

*The Law of Attraction in Action, Episodes I, II, III, IV, V, VI, VII, VIII, IX, X* (2-DVD sets)

*The Teachings of Abraham Master Course Video* (5-DVD set)

*Think and Get Slim* (2-DVD set)

*The Secret Behind "The Secret"?* (Abraham) (2-DVD set)

Please visit Hay House USA: **www.hayhouse.com**®
Hay House Australia: **www.hayhouse.com.au**
Hay House UK: **www.hayhouse.co.uk**
Hay House South Africa: **www.hayhouse.co.za**
Hay House India: **www.hayhouse.co.in**

# The Vortex

## Where the *Law of Attraction* Assembles All Cooperative Relationships

# ESTHER AND JERRY HICKS

(The Teachings of Abraham®)

**HAY HOUSE, INC.**
Carlsbad, California • New York City
London • Sydney • Johannesburg
Vancouver • Hong Kong • New Delhi

*Published and distributed in the United States by:* Hay House, Inc.: www.hayhouse
.com • *Published and distributed in Australia by:* Hay House Australia Pty. Ltd.:
www.hayhouse.com.au • *Published and distributed in the United Kingdom by:* Hay
House UK, Ltd.: www.hayhouse.co.uk • *Published and distributed in the Republic
of South Africa by:* Hay House SA (Pty), Ltd.: www.hayhouse.co.za • *Distributed
in Canada by:* Raincoast: www.raincoast.com • *Published in India by:* Hay House
Publishers India: www.hayhouse.co.in

*Editorial supervision:* Jill Kramer • *Design:* Nick C. Welch

**Library of Congress Cataloging-in-Publication Data**

Hicks, Esther.
 The vortex : where the law of attraction assembles all cooperative relationships / Esther
and Jerry Hicks. -- 1st ed.
     p. cm.
 "The teachings of Abraham."
 ISBN 978-1-4019-1882-8 (pbk. : alk. paper) -- ISBN 978-1-4019-1875-0 (hbk. : alk. paper)
1. Interpersonal relations--Religious aspects. 2. Interpersonal relations--Psychological
aspects. 3. Spirit writings. 4. Spiritual life.  I. Hicks, Jerry. II. Abraham (Spirit) III.
Title.
 BL626.33.H53 2009
 158.2--dc22                                        2009016144


Hardcover ISBN: 978-1-4019-1875-0
Tradepaper ISBN: 978-1-4019-1882-8


12  11  10  09   7  6  5  4
1st edition, September 2009
4th edition, September 2009

Printed in the United States of America

*This book is dedicated to all of you who, in your desire for enlightenment and Well-Being, have asked the questions that this book has answered; and to four delightful children of our children, who are examples of what the book teaches: Laurel (almost 11), Kevin (8), Kate (7), and Luke (almost 4), who are not yet asking because they have not yet forgotten.*

*This book is also dedicated to our friends Louise Hay (founder), Reid Tracy (president), Jill Kramer (editorial director), and the entire staff at Hay House. We are most appreciative of what they have done, and continue to do, to bring to the entire world the Teachings of Abraham.*

# Contents

**PART II: Mating, and the *Law of Attraction*:**
**The Perfect Mate—Getting One, Being One, Attracting One**

## PART III: Sexuality, and the *Law of Attraction:* Sexuality, Sensuality, and the Opinions of Others

**PART IV: Parenting, and the *Law of Attraction:***
**Creating Positive Parent/Child Relationships in a World of Contrast**

**PART V: Self-Appreciation, and the *Law of Attraction:***
**Appreciation, the "Magical" Key to Your Vortex**

**PART VI: Transcript of Abraham Live:**
**A *Law of Attraction* Workshop**

# Preface

# by Jerry Hicks

You are about to delve into the subject of *relationships* from a different perspective, perhaps, than you have previously considered. The teachings contained in this book have to do with aspects of our relationships that are far broader and deeper than "security-loving girl meets freedom-loving boy; they fall in love; they move in together; they work to earn money to acquire stuff; they (in most cases) have children; they continue to work 'full-time' and play 'part-time'; they usually attempt to train their children to match (fit in with) the prevailing cultural, social patterns of 'politically correct' words, behaviors, and beliefs . . . if they live long enough, they retire from working full-time—hopefully to play full-time—and then they move on to . . . ?"

Although the questions and subsequent answers in the book will certainly guide you to a deeper and more practical understanding of those typical family relationships, our intention here is to give you a more conscious awareness of the potential depth and breadth of the vast network of relationships that, on a practical, day-to-day basis, affect your swirling Vortex of natural Well-Being.

At the hub of these teachings of Abraham (not the biblical or presidential *Abraham*) is a profound concept: *the basis of life is freedom; the result of life is expansion—and the purpose of life is joy.*

And so, as you play the words from this book across the life that you have already knowledgeably experienced, the thrust of these teachings will be felt by you as an empowering sense of clarity as you discover concepts whereby you can, more deliberately, create the relationships that feel best to you. *Simply put: regarding every relationship in which you are now, or would like to be, engaged—the Teachings of Abraham are being offered here to guide you to allowing yourself more of what you do want, and less of what you don't want.*

This is the third of four scheduled books in the *Law of Attraction* Series. Our first, *The Law of Attraction: The Basics of the Teachings of Abraham®*, was originally published in book form in 2006; and it quickly became our second book to make the *New York Times* bestseller list.* *Money, and the Law of Attraction,* released in 2008, was the second; and *Spirituality, and the Law of Attraction,* due to be released in 2011, will be the final book in this series.

The material that was to later form our first *Law of Attraction* Series book was first published in 1988 (over 20 years ago) as part of two Special Subjects cassette albums. These original 20 tapes outlined for the listeners practical perceptions of the relationships between the *Universal Law of Attraction* and their finances, careers, bodily conditions, relationships. . . . Our hundreds of questions, and Abraham's forthcoming answers, were focused on 20 practical topics about which people could learn to improve their allowance of their natural state of Well-Being. (If you would like to hear [free] one of those original recordings detailing our introduction to Abraham, you can find our *Introduction to Abraham* recording as a 70-minute free-to-listen-to download at our Website: **www .abraham-hicks.com**; or you can order the CD version from our San Antonio, Texas, business center.)

It was in 2005, while conducting one of our *Law of Attraction* Cruise Seminars, that we were approached by Rhonda Byrne, an Australian television producer. She wanted us to allow her to create an Australian TV series based on the Teachings of Abraham®. And, as a result of our ensuing contractual agreement, Rhonda

---

*Ask and It Is Given,* our first **Amazon.com** bestseller, was published in 2004; and it was followed by four Abraham-Hicks books (all published by Hay House, Inc.) that rapidly reached the *New York Times* bestseller list: *The Amazing Power of Deliberate Intent,* 2005; *The Law of Attraction,* 2006; *The Astonishing Power of Emotions,* 2007; and then, in August of 2008, *Money, and the Law of Attraction: Learning to Attract Wealth, Health, and Happiness* became the first of the Abraham-Hicks books to reach the #1 position on the *New York Times* bestseller list.

brought her Australian film crew on board our 2005 Alaskan *Law of Attraction* cruise and filmed about 14 hours of seminar material. And, as a result, in 2006, the basic tenet of our 1988 album—*The Law of Attraction*—was used as the foundation for the original version of the phenomenally successful DVD movie and subsequent book *The Secret.*

Esther and I don't appear in the revised edition of *The Secret.* We can only be seen in the original version, but between the viral distribution of the original edition and the standard distribution of the revised, "expanded" edition, *The Secret* has added a powerful impetus to the worldwide dissemination of Abraham's teachings regarding the *Universal Law of Attraction.* And we are most appreciative that Rhonda fulfilled her dream of bringing an awareness of Abraham's basic *Law of Attraction* concepts to the world—for, in doing so, she has instilled a *belief,* and evoked an *asking,* in the minds of millions of viewers who have now come to *believe* that they *do* have the ability to achieve better-feeling lives. . . . And so, they are now *asking.* (And Abraham teaches us that "asking" is the first step in the creation process.) And as they have asked, what they have asked for has been given. . . . Their next step now will be to learn to *allow* themselves to receive that which they have been given.

If you were already feeling good when you found this book, then by utilizing these materials, your life can now, by your deliberate intention, spiral toward that which allows you to feel even better. However, if, in this moment, you are feeling less than good—or even if you think your life is as bad as it can possibly get—you can still learn perspectives here that can enable you to allow your life to begin to incrementally improve . . . or, you may be one of those rare ones who, from something you read here, receive a paradigm shift in your Beingness that somehow propels you from a long-term feeling of powerlessness, up into a fresh, long-term joyous alignment with your natural state of Well-Being. And once you reach that state, you will feel like a magnet, attracting to yourself everything—and every relationship—to which you are a Vibrational Match.

I've said that if I receive one practical idea that I can put into practice from a book, a lecture, or a visit with someone, it is well worth spending my time and/or money, because a single new perspective can redirect my thoughts and thereby redirect my life. For instance, a minister friend, Chet Castellaw, said to me back in 1970, "Jerry, you'll never receive the kind of success you're saying you want."

I asked him, "Why not?"

And Chet responded, "Because you are critical of successful people."

"Well," I said, "that's because they lie, cheat, and steal."

And Chet said to me, *"You can be critical of their lying, cheating, and stealing, but you are critical of their <u>success</u> at lying, cheating, and stealing. You can't be critical of huge success and achieve huge success!"*

There it was! Just one idea, a different perspective, that, 38 years ago, I immediately began to act on, which preceded a giant wave of what most would call "coincidental" events that carried me on—joyously—to receiving the essence of everything that I have ever wanted to be, do, or have. . . . And our intention for you is that you will receive ideas from this book that will inspire within you new patterns of thought that will attract to you whatever brings *you* the most of whatever *you* want to be, do, or have.

In this *relationships* book, Abraham* focuses the light of their Broader Perspective to reveal a wide array of *flawed premises* (which most of us are living by) relative to our varied relationships. And as you come upon those false-premise segments ("false," relative to the natural *Laws of the Universe*), if you will superimpose Abraham's perspective over your personal life experience (known only by you), and if you see room for improvement in your life, you will have the opportunity to shift your life—from as good as it is, right now, to whatever you perceive as a better-feeling experience.

Here are a couple of examples of flawed premises under which I operated for many years. Note how those "false" beliefs caused me so much discontent, but even more important, take notice of how a simple change in my perspective led to an immediate major positive change in my life experience:

My mother was born a dyed-in-the-wool nonconformist. I, too, was born as an adamant nonconformist. For over 30 years, Mother

---

*Abraham is considered a group consciousness, so is referred to in the plural.

tried, even quite violently, to get me to conform with what she wanted me to be. Every time I came in contact with her, I tried to vehemently and defensively get her to conform to how *I* wanted her to treat me. Also, I was always a bit embarrassed in public (but somehow proud) of her obvious lack of conformity.

And so, for more than 30 years, every time we came together, we fought! But then, soon after my father died, I adopted a new premise—it just came to me as a complete idea: The "flawed" premise each of us had been operating under for all of those terrible years, was: "If I try hard enough, I can get a 'natural-born nonconformist' to conform." (And how was that working out? It wasn't!) And so, I adopted a new premise: "Since I cannot control Mother—and Mother can't control me—I'll just continue to be the delightful, uncontrollable me that I am; and I will *allow* Mother to be my uncontrollable Mother . . . and, since strangers find Mother's idiosyncrasies entertaining (rather than repulsive), I'll look for and find entertainment in her differences . . ." and we lived happily ever after!

After over 30 years of beatings, restraints, fights . . . I decided to change to a new premise (I didn't ask *her* to change); and, for the next 40 years, we never had another cross word! If it hadn't happened to me, I probably wouldn't have believed it possible—but it did happen.

I'll close this Preface with one more personal "premise" experience: The "abundance" premise of those I associated with in my early days was that those of us who managed to remain poor would always be able to get through a needle's eye, but if we slipped up and were no longer poor, we would get so fat that we wouldn't be able to get through the eye of a needle. (Or something like that—it was a story we were taught in our church.) Another premise that my associates lived by was: "The rich get rich by taking (or somehow keeping) money away from us poor people." For instance, under that premise, if a rich person acquired a luxury automobile, then he or she was leaving less money, or luxury, for us poor, used-economy-car people. And so, operating under that flawed premise, I was unable to comfortably bring myself to potentially impoverish others by buying a luxury vehicle for myself.

And then the idea of *a Universe of never-ending abundance* somehow came to me—another simple thought that I adopted, and adapted, that changed my life, and the lives of those who may have been influenced by my example, in a very dramatic way. My new premise was: "When I buy a series of luxury vehicles, I am creating jobs and redistributing money in a luxurious way. In other words, when I purchase an expensive vehicle, I create work for—and redistribute dollars to—thousands of persons who made the vehicle possible. Some of them are rich, some are on their way to rich, some have no intention of ever being rich, and some believe that being rich will restrict them from entering the eye of a needle. But every one of them has the option of improving their level of joy in some way. And each one of them—whether rich or poor—gained, to some degree, by my purchase of that vehicle: there was the luxury-vehicle salesperson; the dealer; the prep team; the distributor; the wholesaler; the manufacturer; the shareholder; (maybe) the assembly worker; the inventors of the thousands of parts; the designers of the steering wheel, wheel covers, sound systems . . . ; the diggers of the iron ore; the makers of the glass and plastics . . . ; the manufacturers of the paint and tires; the drivers of the many delivery trucks; the manufacturers of the delivery trucks." (Oops! I'd better stop before I get too carried away.)

But I'm sure you get the point I'm making. Once I accepted the premise that *everything is working out for everyone,* then I was able to allow myself to let the floodgates to my financial well-being swing (almost) wide open. And from that decision, I went on to purchase a string of luxury vehicles, always knowing I was passing potential well-being on to anyone who was open to receive it.

And so, as I write this Preface, I am seated at my front desk and Esther is working at her rear office desk in our $2 million tour bus—and I remind myself, often, that this vehicle has brought some degree of pleasure to not only us, but to the thousands of others who had a hand in, and earned money from, its creation.

At any rate, I give you these personal examples to let you feel the long-term power of the adoption of just one good idea; as well as the dynamic value in the recognition, and resolution, of one flawed premise.

This *Vortex* book has been planted with good ideas that are available for you to transplant into your own life experience. And it also recognizes a string of flawed premises, any one of which—if it has been ruling your life—you can now decide to resolve, and replace with a premise that best serves you.

Esther and I are so pleased to participate in this co-creative adventure with you and with Abraham, and we look forward to the joy that you are about to receive as you play with the processes and perspectives embedded in these teachings.

Love ya,
Jerry

❦ ❦ ❦    ❦ ❦ ❦

(**Editor's Note:** Please note that since there aren't always physical English words to perfectly express the Non-Physical thoughts that Esther receives, she sometimes forms new combinations of words, as well as using standard words in new ways—for example, capitalizing them when normally they wouldn't be—in order to express new ways of looking at old ways of looking at life.)

# PART I

# Your Vortex, and the *Law of Attraction:* Learning to Attract Joyous Co-creators

### Learning to Attract Joyous Co-creators

Your life is supposed to feel good to you.

*Before your birth, you knew that the primary component of your physical experience that would offer the greatest value for your personal and collective expansion and joy would be the component of the relationships that you would experience with each other. It was your plan to relish the diversity of your relationships and to choose from them the details that would make up your creations—and here you are.*

Before your birth, as you were making the decision to focus yourself into this Leading Edge time-space reality, it was your powerful intention to enjoy every moment of the process. You understood then, from your Non-Physical perspective, that you are a creator and that you were coming into an environment with enormous potential for joyful, satisfying experiences in creation. You understood that you are a creator, and that the Earth experience would be the perfect platform from which you would launch numerous satisfying creations—and here you are.

*Before your birth into your physical body, you knew that once you were here, you would be surrounded by others and that your relationships with those others would be the primary source of the contrast you would live. You understood, also, that these contrasting relationships would provide the very basis of your personal expansion, as well as the very basis of your enormous contribution to Eternal expansion, and you eagerly welcomed your interaction with all of them—and here you are.*

There was nothing in your plan about being here that included struggle or hardship. You did not believe that you were coming into physical form to right past wrongs, or to fix a broken world, or even to evolve (in the sense that you were currently *lacking* in something). Instead, you knew this physical experience would be an environment that would provide a balance of contrast from which you would personally make increasingly improved choices that would add to your own expansion as well as to the collective expansion of *All-That-Is*. You knew that this world of contrast would induce in you the expansion that literally puts the Eternalness into Eternity; and your appreciation for the contrasting environment on planet Earth was enormous, for you understood that contrast is the basis of expansion, and that the expansion would be joyous—and here you are.

Before your birth into your physical body, you knew the value of variety and of diversity, for you understood that every new preference, desire, or idea would be born from that contrast. And you knew that this contrast not only provided the literal basis for expansion, but also the basis for your joyful experience. And, most of all, you knew that your joyful experience would be the ultimate reason for every part of every part of every part of all of this Beingness. You knew that it all exists for the joyful moments that would constantly explode into your awareness along the way—and here you are.

Before your birth, you understood *contrast* to be the variety from which you would make your choices. You knew that your surrounding environment would be like a dining buffet spread out before you, from which you would choose, and that nothing about that environment was permanent because your constant new choices would cause it to continually change—and here you are.

Before your birth, you understood that all choices are made by giving attention to something. You knew that you were about to focus your Consciousness into a physical body and into a physical time-space reality; and that you would make your selections from the contrasting buffet of choices that would surround you by your attention, focus, or thought—and here you are.

Before your birth, you understood that the Earth environment, like all environments—physical and Non-Physical—is a Vibrationally based environment, which is managed by the *Law of*

*Attraction* (that which is like unto itself, is drawn); and you knew that your attention to any subject was your invitation for your personal participation with it—and here you are.

Before your birth, in considering your physical experience on planet Earth, you did not request to be born into an environment of sameness or agreement, where all of the variety had already been considered and all of the decisions about how life should be lived had been made, for you were a powerful creator who was coming forth for the purpose of making your own decisions and of creating your own joyful experience. You knew that *diversity* would be your best friend, and that *conformity,* on every level, would be the opposite. You literally dived in, in eagerness to find your bearings and to then begin to explore, from your own personal, important, and powerful viewpoint, your contrasting surroundings, from which you would carve out your creations—and here you are.

Many people express concern and frustration—and, at times, anger and resentment—that they did not retain conscious awareness of these prebirth decisions, but we submit that you arrived in your physical body with something even more important intact: *you were born with a personal Guidance System to help you to know— every step (or thought) along the way—when you are diverging from your prebirth understanding of life, and when you are on track.*

It is our desire that you become consciously aware of your own *Guidance System* so that you can explore this new frontier of creation in alignment with the stability of your Non-Physical knowledge.

It is our desire to help you consciously reconnect with *who-you-really-are* and to help you replace myriad false premises—which you have erroneously picked up along your physical trail—with Universal, *Law*-based premises of life.

*It is our desire to help you to solve the mystery of seemingly impossible relationships; to sort out the details of sharing your planet with billions of others; to rediscover the beauty of differences; and, most of all, to re-establish the most important relationship of all: your relationship with the Eternal, Non-Physical Source that is really you—and here we are.*

## Life Is about Our Relationships

*You will never find yourself in a point in time when the subject of relationships is not an active part of your <u>now</u> experience, for everything you perceive or notice or know is because of your relationship with something else. Without a comparative experience, you would be unable to perceive or focus any kind of understanding within yourself. Therefore, it is accurate to say that without relationships you could not exist at all.*

It is our desire that an even greater awareness of *who-you-are* will awaken within you by reading this book, as you begin to explore the variety of relationships that you are already living.

It is our desire that you experience an enhanced appreciation of your planet; your body; your family; your friends; your enemies; your government; your systems; your food; your finances; your animals; your work; your play; your purpose; your Source; your Soul; your past, your future, and your present. . . .

*It is our desire that you come to remember that every relationship is Eternal and that once it has been established, it is a part of your Vibrational makeup forevermore, and that, in your powerful now—where all that you have become converges with all that you are now becoming—you hold the power to create.*

Often, when you observe an unwanted or unpleasant experience, you believe that you are not personally a part of it, but instead a distant, dissociated, unattached observer of it; but that is never the case. *Your observation of a situation—no matter how remote you believe yourself to be—makes you a co-creative partner of the experience.*

Over time, as you have interacted with one another, many of you have arrived at collective preferences about how life should be lived; and while you have come nowhere close to an agreement about what the appropriate way to live is, still, on the myriad subjects that *you* are experiencing, you continue to try to convince others to accept the preferences that *you* most prefer.

## Find Alignment First and Then Take Action

In every society of the vast number of societies on your planet today, you have instituted rules, requirements, taboos, laws—along with a great variety of rewards and punishments for conforming or not conforming—as each society seems determined to sort into separate piles the *wanted* from the *unwanted.* And although you work very hard at the sorting process, the piles continue to shift around; and you never come even close to a consensus of *wanted* and *unwanted, right* and *wrong, good* and *bad.*

It is our desire that, as a result of just reading this one book, you will never again require global, community, or even a partner's agreement in order to find your confidence, direction, and power. *We want you to remember that the need for agreement from others comes from a basis of misunderstanding of the <u>Laws of the Universe</u> and runs counter to <u>who-you-really-are.</u>*

It is our desire that, by understanding your own personal *Guidance System,* you will return to alignment with the power that flows to you and through you. For by your finding agreement with the power that flows forth from within you, the harmony that you seek on all other levels and all other subjects—and with all others—will then (and only then) be possible.

Most people would deem it unwise to load a big clumsy truck, which has a very bad suspension system and a steering mechanism so worn-out that it is almost impossible to keep the truck on the road, with their most precious cargo. Or, most people would deem it unwise to gather a load of precious glass antiques and put them in the carrying basket of the bicycle that their five-year-old son is taking on his first bicycle ride today. Or, most people would deem it unwise to carry a sack containing their life's savings and all of their favorite jewelry and then walk out onto the iced-over lake before they were sure that the ice was actually strong enough to hold their weight.

In other words, it always makes sense to first find fundamental stability before embarking on any journey, especially those journeys that matter most to you. And yet, as people interact with one another on important subjects, they commonly plunge headlong into conversations and decisions and behaviors before they have achieved any sense of true stability, and then the return to stability is often very long in coming. And often, once out of balance, they stumble into the next and then the next and then the next out-of-control experience. *Through the examples in this book, it is our desire to help you remember the art of alignment first—then action. Alignment first—then conversation. Alignment first—then interaction. Alignment first—then anything else.*

People sometimes say, "Think before you speak." A wise intention, but we would take it further. We would suggest, *"Think—and then evaluate the value of that thought by noticing how it feels; and do that often enough that you know, without question, that you are in alignment—then speak, then act, then interact."*

Someone who takes the time to understand their relationship with Source, who actively seeks alignment with their Broader Perspective, who deliberately seeks and finds alignment with *who-they-really-are,* is more charismatic, more attractive, more effective, and more powerful than a group of millions who have not achieved that alignment.

The historical masters and healers whom you revere understood the value of this personal alignment. And in this book about *relationships,* we submit to you: *There is no relationship of greater importance to achieve than the relationship between you, in your physical body, right here and now, and the Soul/Source/God from which you have come. If you tend to that relationship first and foremost, you will then, and only then, have the stable footing to proceed into other relationships. Your relationship with your own body; your relationship with money; your relationship with your parents, children, grandchildren, the people you work with, your government, your world . . . will all fall swiftly and easily into alignment once you tend to this fundamental, primary relationship first.*

### Are We Living Under Flawed Premises?

You may have chosen to read this book because of a particular issue that you are having with someone in your life, and we want you to know that the answers you are looking for *are* contained within the covers of this book. If you were to read the Contents pages at the beginning of this book, you might even be able to pinpoint the specific relationship that you most want to address. And we understand how tempting it is to simply turn to those pages to find your answer—and if you were to do that, you *would* find your answer, and it would be the *right* answer—but if, instead of doing that, you will systematically read through the pages of this book in the order that they are written, then when you come to the section of the book that pertains to the relationship issue you are most interested in soothing, it is our promise to you: the soothing will be greater, the solution easier to understand, and your relationship issue will be more quickly reconciled.

Whether you read this book in one sitting or over a period of several days, an important transformation will take place within you: *Flawed premises that you have picked up along your physical trail will fall by the wayside, one by one, and you will return to the understanding that is at the core of that which you are. And when that happens, not only will you begin to understand every current and past relationship, but the benefit that every relationship has given you will become immediately apparent to you.*

Without exception, the flawed premise or unstable footing that most people stand on is because they care more about what someone else is thinking about them than how they themselves are feeling. So, over time, by interacting with many others (who also want to feel better and have trained those around them to offer behavior that does make them temporarily feel better—that is, "Don't please you, but instead please me"—that is, "Don't you dare be selfish and satisfy yourself, but instead please me"), they have lost sight of their own Guidance and have become further and further separated from *who-they-are*. And so, they feel worse and worse as time goes on, and so they come to incorrect conclusion after incorrect conclusion until they are completely lost.

It seems logical that an exposing of those flawed premises would clear things up and put them back on their path of Well-Being. However, when you are standing in the middle of a flawed premise, focusing upon the results of it, you are usually so engulfed in the

Vibration of it—and therefore so actively attracting because of it—that you cannot see its inherent flaw. It does not feel false when your life continues to unfold in the way you "believed" it would.

In order to discover or understand a false or flawed premise, you have to stand back far enough and reconnect with *who-you-really-are* before you can see it. In other words, if you were to interact with an unkind (disconnected) person who told you continually that you are not smart, at first you would take issue with the idea. The negative emotion you would feel is because the words *You are not smart* are so contradictory to the true knowledge of your Source. *But if you were to hear this again and again, until you yourself began to believe and repeat the false premise, now your own activation of the contradictory Vibration would interfere with your own sense of intelligence, and you would begin to attract evidence of your lack of intelligence, in effect proving the false premise to be true. It becomes increasingly hard for you to call this a "false" premise when the evidence seems to be telling you that it is true. Over time you come to believe it is true.*

The good news in all of this is that whenever you know what you *do not* want, an equal and proportionate desire for what you *do* want erupts from you, and a rocket of desire shoots forward into your Vibrational Reality. In other words, the potential for a greatly improved experience is always born from an unwanted experience; and, in time (whenever the resistance ceases), the improvement will come.

We write this book so that you can allow your improvement sooner rather than later, or sooner rather than not in this lifetime—but in any event, future generations will benefit dramatically from the contrast your current generation is living. It is our desire to assist you in unraveling and releasing these erroneous, incorrect, unhelpful beliefs, to help you free yourself from the bondage of these false premises. We want you to remember *who-you-really-are* and to stand in that fresh light, in that fresh place of attracting on all subjects.

Most people who are in the midst of observing something unwanted in another person believe that if the unwanted condition were not there to be observed, they would not be observing it.

Most people who are in the midst of observing something unwanted in another person believe that the discomfort they are feeling is because of the unpleasant condition that is being offered by the other person, and that if the other person would no longer offer the unpleasant condition, then they (the ones observing) would feel better.

Most people who are in the midst of observing something unwanted in another person believe that if they could control the behavior of the other—through influence, persuasion, coercion, rules, laws, or threat of punishment—in the gaining control of unwanted situations, they would feel better.

Most people believe that control of conditions and of others is the key to feeling better, but that belief is the greatest flawed premise of all. The belief that if you could get all circumstances to change so that your observation of them would then feel good to you defies the *Laws of the Universe,* as well as your reason for being here. *It was never your intention to control everything around you. It was your intention to control the direction of your thought.*

Throughout this book, we will identify a series of flawed premises that are at the heart of the confusion and distortion of your physical reality. It is our desire that, as you make your way through the pages of this book, you will be able to release the flawed premises that contradict your Broader knowing so that you can return to the natural state of allowing the Well-Being of your life to flow to you.

## Gaining a Clear View by Stepping Back

While we are eager to rendezvous with you, right where you are, in order to help you improve every relationship that is currently active in your experience, it will be of value for you to first relax and walk with us down the path of the usual human interactions experienced from the time of physical birth until the time of physical death. Of course, you are different in many ways from one another—but, for the most part, no matter when you were born or what part of the world you live in, there are typical, predominant relationship patterns that are really worth considering. This overview of the evolution of the relationships that you experience as physically focused humans has the potential of helping you to realize—no matter what phase of human evolution you are currently focused within—a myriad of flawed beliefs that humans have been passing on to one another for a very long time. By stepping back from the immediacy of your current experience and seeing the full spectrum of your physical human life experience in the way we present it here, you will gain a clear view of your life's purpose, and you will discover an immediate stable footing that will set you on your course for joy for the rest of this life experience.

### Before Your Birth into This Physical Body

Before you focused a part of your Consciousness into the physical body that you now recognize as *you*, you were an intelligent, clear, happy, nonresistant Consciousness eager for this new experience into which you were emerging. Before your birth, the only relationship you experienced was your relationship with your Source; but since you were, at that time, Non-Physical, and therefore nonresistant, you experienced no discernible separation, and therefore no discernible "relationship," between you and Source. *You were Source.*

In other words, while you have fingers and toes and arms and legs, you do not see them as separate Beings. You see them as a part of you. So you usually do not try to describe your *relationship* with your leg, because you understand that your leg is you. And so, before your physical birth, you were Vibrationally intertwined with *Source,* or with what humans often call *God,* but the full integration of you with *God* was such that there was no relationship between the two—because you were all One.

### The Moment of Your Birth

In the moment of your birth, a part of the Consciousness that is you focused itself into your physical body, and your first relationship began: the relationship between the physical you and the Non-Physical You.

Here we come upon a significant flawed premise, or misunderstanding, of many—in fact, most—of our physical human friends:

> **Flawed Premise #1:** *I am either physical or*
> *Non-Physical, either dead or alive.*

> *Many people do not understand that they existed before their*
> *physical birth. Many others believe that if they existed in the*
> *Non-Physical before their birth, the Non-Physical part of them*
> *ceased to be once they were born into this body. In other words,*
> *"I am either Non-Physical or physical, either dead or alive."*

We want you to remember that while you are focused here in this Leading Edge body in this Leading Edge time, the Eternal, Non-Physical, older, wiser, larger part of you remains Non-Physically focused. And because that Non-Physical part of you exists, and because *You* exist, there is an Eternal, undeniable relationship between those two important aspects of you.

This relationship (this Vibrational relationship) that exists between the physical you and the Non-Physical You is significant for many reasons:

1. The emotions that you feel (your *Emotional Guidance System*) are because of the relationship between these two Vibrational parts of you.

2. As you reach for new thoughts and expansion, out here on the Leading Edge of life, you have the benefit of the stable knowledge of your Non-Physical counterpart.

3. As you reach for new thoughts and expansion, out here on the Leading Edge of life, the Non-Physical part of you has the benefit of the expansion that you carve out of your physical experience.

4. Every other relationship you have (that is, with other people, with animals, with your own body, with money, with concepts and ideas, with life itself) is profoundly affected by this all-important relationship between *you* and *You.*

### Your Relationship with Your Parents

Of course, your physical parents are of great significance to you, for if it were not for their relationship with each other, you would not exist in your current physical form. But there are many misunderstandings, or what we are calling *flawed premises,* around your relationships with your parents.

From your Non-Physical vantage point, you understood that your physical parents would be your important avenue into physical experience, and that you would be born into a stable enough environment to be able to get your physical footing. You knew that your parents, or others like them, would receive you and introduce you to your new environment. You knew that there would be a time of acclimation, and you felt enormous appreciation for those who would welcome you.

You understood that your parents, who were already acclimated to their physical environment, would help you in finding food, shelter, and physical stability. But you did not intend to look to them to determine your life's purpose for you, or for guidance about the correctness or effectiveness of your physical journey. In fact, from your Non-Physical perspective before your birth, you knew that *your personal guidance* would be more intact (and therefore more effective) on the day that you were born than would be the guidance of the adults who would greet you. In other words, when you were first born into your physical body, the relationship between you and You (your Non-Physical *Inner Being*) was such that you were nearly still that *One* Pure, Positive Energy.

But in those very first new days in your physical body, you began to experience a gradual shift in your own Consciousness (just as you knew you would) as you began to garner your personal perspective (from your *physical* vantage point) of your new Earth environment. And in that process, your Energy, or Consciousness, became two instead of one. In other words, as the new infant in your mother's arms, you had two Vibrational vantage points active within you—*and so, you then began to feel emotions.*

Since you just came from an environment where you had absolute knowledge of the Well-Being of the Universe and of planet Earth and of *All-That-Is,* when your mother held you and worried about you—you felt uncomfortable. When your parents felt overwhelmed with their lives—you felt uncomfortable. When they gazed at you in pure love and appreciation—you felt the alignment of their Beings, and you felt comfort. But, even in your infancy, you remembered that it was not their job to shine their alignment on you. You remembered, even then—even before you could talk or walk—that it was not their job to provide a haven of comfort and aligned Energy for you. You knew it was *your* job, and you knew you would figure it out. And, meanwhile, you were able to easily withdraw back into the alignment of your Oneness—and so you slept. Often.

You came into this physical environment knowing that you would be surrounded by *contrast* right from the beginning, and that this contrast would provide the nucleus of the creation of your own life experience. You understood that just by being present in this Earth environment, you would automatically find your own preferences, and that both *wanted* and *unwanted* aspects would be of benefit to you. And, most of all, you knew that you would be the one (the only one) who would (or could) choose for you. However, by the time you came into the life experience of your parents, they had (in most cases) all but forgotten that about you. Which brings us to another flawed premise:

> **Flawed Premise #2:** *My parents, because they were here long before I was born, and because they are my parents, know better than I do what is right or wrong for me.*

*You did not intend to use the opinions of your parents to measure against your beliefs, desires, or actions in order to determine the appropriateness of them. Instead, you knew (and still remembered, long after you were born) that it was the relationship between the opinion (or knowledge) of the Source within you and your current thoughts, in any moment, that would offer you perfect guidance in the form of emotions. You did not intend to replace your <u>Emotional Guidance System</u> with the opinions of your parents even if they were in harmony with their <u>Emotional Guidance System</u> in the moment of their trying to guide you. It was much more important to you to recognize the existence of your own <u>Guidance System,</u> and to utilize it, than to be deemed correct by, or to find approval from, others.*

*Much of the imbalance that people feel long after they leave the immediate environment of their childhood home stems from the impossible effort of replacing their own <u>Guidance System</u> by seeking approval from their parents.* Your feeling of freedom is trampled whenever you try to align with the opinion of someone outside of you (that is, your parents) rather than aligning with the Vibration that comes forth from within you (that is, your *Inner Being*). Of course, it is possible to have a wonderful, effective relationship with your parents if you first find the alignment between *you* and *You*. But, unless you have achieved alignment between *you* and *You,* no other relationship can be a good one.

## Your Relationship with Your Siblings

Whether you were the first child your parents welcomed into your childhood home or if you came after another who was already there, multiple children certainly can change the dynamics of your parental relationships. In most relationship settings, the more people involved, the more the possibility that personal misalignment will occur; but that does not have to be the case.

Often the family dynamics are as follows: Your mother and father have not been consciously aware of their own *Guidance*

*Systems,* and so they do not offer to themselves—or to each other—consistent patterns of alignment. They often believe that it is up to you to alter your behavior in order to positively affect their experience. So, not long after you have settled into their life experience, they attempt to train you into patterns of behavior that *they* have deemed favorable. But, they are attempting the impossible. Instead of achieving their alignment with *who-they-really-are,* they are asking *you* to behave in a way that makes *them* feel better. That is what *conditional love* is: "If you will change your behavior or condition, then as I observe it, I will feel better. So I am giving you the responsibility for the way I feel."

When the second child enters the mix, not only is there now more behavior for your parents to attempt to control, but an even more confusing thing occurs for you: now, not only are you considering your own behavior in relationship to your parents' response to what you are doing, but you are observing the way your parents are responding to the behavior of the other child. *The potential for distortion and confusion exponentially expands with each new person who enters the mix.*

*Trying to achieve your proper personal behavior is not possible through trying to adjust to the desires and demands of the people you live with. There is simply too much variety in personality, interest, intention, and life purpose coming in for you to sort it out on a behavior level. But there is something you can do that will bring each of these relationships into perspective and satisfaction for you: <u>Seek alignment between you and You, first, before you engage with any other. And never ask for a behavioral change from any other to use as your basis of improved emotion or perspective. There are simply too many moving parts, and you will not succeed.</u>*

## Our Vortex, and the *Law of Attraction*

It is our desire that, through reading this book, you will discover a new sense of clarity about how your physical life experience fits into the greater scheme of things. We want you to remember *who-you-really-are* and why you are here in this physical body. Most of all, it is our desire that you regain your sense of worthiness and absolute Well-Being; and, it is our desire that you understand the important role that you fulfill by being here in the Leading Edge, contrast-filled time-space reality.

Before you came into this body, you were Non-Physical Energy; and from that Non-Physical perspective of Source, you extended or focused a part of your Consciousness forward into your physical time, physical Earth, and physical body. And when you were born into this body, achieving awareness through your physical senses of your new surroundings—the Consciousness known as *you* became two specific aspects: the Non-Physical part of you and the physical part of you.

Some refer to their Non-Physical aspect as their *Soul* or *Source;* and while we prefer labels like *Inner Being, Broader Non-Physical Perspective,* or *who-you-really-are,* there is an even more important distinction that we would like you to understand: *both the Non-Physical and physical aspects of you exist at the same time.* Most people acknowledge that some aspect of them existed prior to their physical birth, and most believe that after their physical death, they will again be Non-Physical, but something quite different from that is occurring: *You are extensions of Source Energy, and when you became physically focused, your Non-Physical aspect did not cease to be. In fact, your Non-Physical aspect began to expand because of the existence and experience of your physical aspect.*

It was your clear intention to come forth into your magnificent physical body and to interact with the variety of intentions and beliefs and desires of others upon your planet for the purpose of expansion. You understood that by your exposure to the variety that surrounds you, on all subjects, you would naturally come to specific conclusions of improvement. You knew that by living an unpleasant experience, a request for an improved experience would be born. You knew that a request, or asking, or desire would emanate from you Vibrationally; and that your *Inner Being* would be aware of your new request and would follow it and focus upon it and become it. You knew that your *Inner Being* would immediately become the Vibrational equivalent of every request that your physical environment inspired.

And so, if you can now turn your attention to the idea of your expanded *Inner Being,* who stands as the culmination of all that you have lived, who emits a Vibration that expresses the whole of that which you have become—then you will more fully understand who your *Inner Being* is and how the physical aspect of you has added to that expansion.

*We want you to realize that while you are focused in your physical body, thinking thoughts, speaking words, involved in action . . . at the same time there is a Non-Physical aspect of you who exists in the Non-Physical realm from which you have come—and the Non-Physical aspect of you has expanded because of your physical experiences.*

Many people refer to their physical life experience as *reality.* You decipher your physical reality through your physical senses, and as you look around your planet at the places and people and experiences, you pronounce it *reality.* We want you to understand that even though you are seeing and hearing and tasting and smelling and touching the evidence of your physical reality, it is much more than the flesh, blood, and bone reality that you believe it is. *Everything that you perceive here in your physical environment is Vibration, and the life you are living is your Vibrational interpretation.*

The powerful *Law of Attraction* is at the root of everything that you experience; and the stable, never-changing, always-accurate premise of this *Law* is: *that which is like unto itself, is drawn.*

When you give thought to something, you begin the attraction process of the essence of that subject into your own life experience. Once you have activated a thought-Vibration within yourself by giving your attention to the subject, the progression of expansion occurs. In other words, the more attention you give to any subject, the more active the Vibration of that subject is within you. And the longer that occurs, the more powerful the attraction is, until, eventually, you will have irrefutable evidence in your own experience of that active Vibration. All things that happen in your experience come because of the requests that you are sending out with your thoughts.

*The Law of Attraction is the Universal manager of all Vibration, which expands to everything that exists through the Universe. And so, at the same time that the Law of Attraction is responding to the Vibrational* *content of your physical thoughts, it is also responding to the Vibrational content of your <u>Inner Being.</u>*

We want to draw your attention toward that powerful, Non-Physical aspect of you and the effect that the *Law of Attraction* has upon it: Each time your physical life experience causes you to ask for something, a Vibrational, rocketlike request shoots forward and is received by your *Inner Being* and becomes the Vibrational, expanded version of your request. In order to help you get a sense of that process of expansion, we have called it your *Vibrational Escrow* or your *Vibrational Reality.* It is the furthermost, expanded version of you.

*In the same way that the <u>Law of Attraction</u> is responding to the thoughts, words, and actions that you are offering here in your physical reality, the <u>Law of Attraction</u> is always responding powerfully to your Vibrational Reality. When the <u>Law of Attraction,</u> the Universal manager of all Vibrations, responds to the clarity of Vibration offered by your newly expanded <u>Inner Being,</u> the result is a powerful swirling Vortex of attraction.*

So here is this Vortex of becoming—a Vortex that contains all of the requests, all of the amended requests, each and every detail of each and every asking that has emanated from you—and the *Law of Attraction* is responding to that. Envision this swirling, swirling, swirling Vortex and the power of attraction that is amassed as the *Law of Attraction* responds to this pure, nonresisted, focused desire. *The Vortex is literally drawing in all things necessary for the completion of every request it contains. All cooperative components are being summoned and are coming for the completion of these creations, for the answering of these questions, for the solutions to these problems.*

The purpose of this book is not only to help you remember the process of creation—and remember the Pure, Positive Energy platform from which you have come—but to help you remember the power of this Vortex and to remind you of your *Emotional Guidance System* so that you can *consciously* and *deliberately* achieve the Vibrational frequency of your Vortex.

The purpose of this book is:

- To help you remember *who-you-really-are*

- To help you remember the purpose of your physical experience

- To restore your feeling of self-appreciation for what you are accomplishing here in your physical body

- To help you remember that you are, first and foremost, a Vibrational Being

- To help you remember that there is a Non-Physical aspect of you that exists now, also

- To help you be aware of the relationship between the two Vibrational aspects of you

- To help point your awareness consistently toward the swirling Vortex of Creation, which contains all that you desire and all that you have become.

In short, this book is written to help you get into your Vortex.

*Everyone who turns up in your life—from the people you call friends or lovers, to the people you call enemies or strangers—comes in response to your <u>Vibrational asking.</u> You not only invite the person, but you also invite the personality traits of the person.* Many people have a difficult time accepting this as they think of many of the unwanted characteristics of people in their lives. They argue that they would never have asked for something so unwanted to come into their experience, for they believe that "asking" for something means "asking for something wanted." But by "asking," we mean offering a matching Vibration. . . . *We know that many of the relationships or experiences you have attracted, you would not have <u>deliberately</u> attracted if you had been doing it on purpose, but much of your attraction is not done by deliberate intent, but rather by default. . . . It is important to understand that you get what you think about, whether you want it or not. And chronic thoughts about unwanted things invite, or ask for, matching experiences. The <u>Law of Attraction</u> makes it so.*

Relationships, or co-creating with others, is responsible for nearly all of the contrast in your life. They are responsible for the troubles of your life *and* your greatest pleasures. But, most important of all, the relationships that you experience with one another are the basis of the majority of the expansion that you achieve; and because of that, it is accurate to also say that the relationships of your life are the reason for the potential for your joy—or your pain—in any moment in time. Simply put, if someone had not prodded you into more expansion, you could not feel the pain of not keeping up with that expansion. The interaction, intertwining, and co-creation of relationships enhances your individual experience enormously. *Your greatest joys and your greatest sorrows come from the basis of your relationships, but you have more control over whether you experience joy or sorrow than you realize.*

### The Powerful, Eternal, Universal *Law of Attraction*

The powerful *Law of Attraction* (that which is like unto itself, is drawn) is at the root of everything that you experience. So, when you give thought to something, you begin the attraction process of the essence of that subject into your own life experience. Once you have activated a thought-Vibration within yourself by giving your attention to the subject, the progression of expansion occurs. In other words, the more attention you give to any subject, the more active the Vibration of that subject is within you; and the longer that occurs, the more powerful the attraction is . . . until, eventually, you will have irrefutable evidence in your own experience of that active Vibration. All things that happen in your experience come because of the requests that you are sending out with your thoughts.

*Remember that whether you are thinking about <u>wanted</u> things or <u>unwanted</u> things, you are still sending out a "request" to attract more things like the subject of your thought. And all things that happen to you—all people, things, experiences, situations that come to you—come in response to your Vibrational invitation.*

*The culmination of relationships and circumstances and events that you draw to you is utterly accurate in its response to your Vibrational requests. Noticing how things are turning out for you is one very clear way of understanding which Vibrational requests you are emanating, because you always get the essence of what you are thinking about, whether you want it or not.* We call that *post-manifestational awareness:* vibrating with no deliberate direction of thought, but then noticing the results of the thoughts only after they have manifested into something real or tangible, such as a low balance in your bank account, an unwanted physical condition, or an unpleasant relationship.

It is possible to become aware of the attracting of an unwanted situation and to head it off before it comes into full realization in your experience by becoming aware of, and utilizing, the wonderful *Emotional Guidance System* you were born with. But most people indiscriminately give attention to whatever is in their view, and then accept the inevitability of their emotional responses to those thoughts. They accept that there are bad things out there in the world, and when they focus upon those bad things, they expect to feel bad—and they do. Rarely do they understand the important reason for their bad feeling, but we will state it simply for you here:

*When you focus upon a subject or situation and you feel bad, it is not the subject or the situation that is the reason for your bad feeling. You feel bad because the thoughts have caused a Vibrational separation in you. In other words, you have chosen to give your attention to something that the Source within you is not giving attention to.* And it is with good reason that the Source within you is not giving attention to the thing that makes you feel bad when *you* do. *Source understands the power of attraction and does not want to add to the creation of unwanted things; and when you do, you feel bad. Every time.*

And, conversely, when you think thoughts during which you feel passionate or happy or loving or eager, you are choosing thoughts in which the larger part of you is also completely immersed; but instead of causing a separation between you and your Source, you are now creating a partnership or relationship with power and clarity and Well-Being.

There is no understanding on any subject that is of greater value to you than the understanding of the existence of your personal

*Emotional Guidance System.* When you are aware of the existence of your two significant Vibrational perspectives and how they relate to one another, you consciously hold the key to your joyful Deliberate Creation. And without that understanding, you are a bit like a small cork bobbing atop a raging sea, blown by the current and the wind, out of your personal control.

You could say that, in any moment, you really only have access to two emotions: one that feels better and one that feels worse. If you will make a determination that, from wherever you stand and no matter what you are focusing upon, you will reach for the best-feeling thought you can find from where you are, then you will develop an ongoing relationship with your *Inner Being,* with Source, and with all that you desire—and your life will become consistently joyous. That was your plan: to sift through variety, come to personal clarity about what you prefer on topic after topic, and then to come into alignment with your eternally evolving self.

### Are We Tolerating Others, or Allowing Them?

**Jerry:** But since we are all so different, it doesn't seem to me that there is much chance of us ever coming together on common agreements about how we should all live life.

**Abraham:** We agree. And it would be a very boring place if that were the case.

**Jerry:** Since we are all different and we want different things, how can we move forward without feeling the pain of having to put up with, or tolerate, those differences in others?

**Abraham:** Your pain, or negative emotion, is not because of your disagreement with another person. It is always about the disagreement between *you* and *You.* If you will withdraw your attention from the unwanted and put it upon something you *do* like, your pain will subside. As you focus longer still upon something that you *do* want, not only will you no longer feel pain, but you will feel positive emotion, such as interest or eagerness or happiness.

**Jerry:** But since we are all somehow connected, how can a person learn to allow the uncomfortable things that are occurring in other people's lives?

**Abraham:** All understanding comes through the comparative living of life. And by "comparative," we mean weighing all current observations against the true knowledge that emanates from your Source. From your Broader Perspective, you know that attention to unwanted things adds to them—and so, the Source part of you withdraws attention from all things that are unwanted. When you, in your physical body, give your attention to unwanted things, you cause a disparity in the Vibrational relationship between *you* and *You,* and your negative emotion is your indication of that discord or lack of alignment. And in that absence of alignment, you are of no value to the person you are worrying about or angry with. And when you think about it, since you cannot control the circumstances of the lives of others, you have no real choice—if it is your desire to be happy—other than to withdraw your attention from their uncomfortable situation.

**Jerry:** But won't others feel abandoned if we withdraw our attention from the pain they are experiencing? Don't we have some responsibility to help those in need?

**Abraham:** Here is an opportunity to begin to understand a basic flawed premise of your society:

> **Flawed Premise #3:** *If I push hard enough against unwanted things, they will go away.*

You live in a Universe that is based upon the *Law of Attraction.* That means that this is an inclusion-based Universe, not an exclusion-based Universe. In other words, in an inclusion-based, attraction-based Universe, there simply is no such thing as "no." When you look at something wanted and you say "yes" to it, you are including it in your Vibration; and it then becomes a part of your Vibrational offering, which means it is a part of your point of attraction, which means—it begins to come to you. But when you shout "no" at something, you are including *it* in your Vibration, also, so it then becomes a part of your Vibrational offering, which means it is a part of your point of attraction, which means—it begins to come to you.

You are of no advantage whatsoever to anyone who has your negative attention. When you observe something in another that causes you to feel bad while you are observing it, your negative emotion is your indicator that you are adding to something unwanted. In the early stages of negative emotion, you merely feel discomfort, but if you continue your focus upon unwanted things, unwanted things will begin to appear in your own experience in increasingly prominent ways.

In every conscious moment, your point of attraction is active, which means that the *Law of Attraction* is responding to your active Vibration and you are in the state of becoming more. Your emotions are your indication of whether you are becoming *more* like the positive, uplifting Being of your *Source* or whether you are becoming *more* of the opposite of that. *You cannot stand still. If you are awake, you are in the process of expansion.*

*Whenever you know what you <u>do not</u> want, you always know more clearly what you <u>do</u> want, so in a poignant moment of awareness of another person's undesirable situation, you automatically launch your version of an improved situation forward into your Vibrational Reality. Now, your work, your value to that person, your value to yourself, your natural state of being . . . is to give your undivided attention to the idea of improvement that has hatched from your interaction/observation. And as you learn to do that, not only will you be of increasing value to others, but you will see how your relationships with others add immeasurably to your own becoming.*

## Learning the *Art of Allowing*

**Jerry:** You have spoken to us often of the *Art of Allowing*. Is that what you are speaking of here?

**Abraham:** Yes. The *Art of Allowing* is what you want most to understand, because, in deliberately applying it, you "allow" yourself to be all that you have become. And anything less than the allowing of you to be *You* feels less good. In other words, every contrasting experience causes an expansion of *who-you-are* because the larger Non-Physical part of you always moves to that point of farthest expansion. But if you continue to look back to the events or circumstances or reasons that caused the expansion, you then hold yourself in opposition to the very expansion. You disallow it—and then you feel bad.

The *Art of Allowing* is simply your allowing yourself, by virtue of your deliberately chosen thoughts, to keep up with the expansion of yourself. And since the expansion is happening—because the contrast of your time-space reality insists that it does—if you are to be happy, you have no other choice than to keep up.

The Broader Non-Physical part of you, to whom you have an Eternal relationship, is one who loves. When you are not loving, you are not practicing the *Art of Allowing*.

The Broader Non-Physical part of you is one who knows your worthiness. When you feel unworthy, you are not practicing the *Art of Allowing*.

Here is an opportunity to begin to understand another basic flawed premise of your society:

**Flawed Premise #4:** *I have come here to live the right way of life and to influence others to the same right way of living. And what feels right to me must be the right way of living for all.*

You did not come into this physical experience intending to take all of the ideas that exist and whittle them down to a handful of good ideas that everyone agrees on. In fact, the opposite was your intention. You said, "I will go forth, into a sea of contrast; and from it, more ideas will be born." You understood that joyous expansion would be born from diversity.

*Since everyone wants to feel good, but there are so many things that others are doing that, as you observe them, you do not feel are good, it is easy to understand how you would come to the conclusion that your path to feeling good is through influencing or controlling the behavior of others. But as you attempt to control them (through influence or coercion), you discover that not only can you not contain them—but your attention to them brings more like them into your experience.* Your current society is waging a war against illegal drugs, a war against poverty, a war against crime, a war against teenage pregnancy, a war against cancer, a war against AIDS, a war against terrorism . . . and all of them are getting bigger. You simply cannot get to where you want to be by controlling or eliminating the unwanted.

And who among you gets to decide which way of living is the "right" one, anyway? Is the largest group the one that holds that "knowledge," or is the group with the greatest capacity to kill the other groups the one who is "right"? Do poor people have the answer? Do rich people hold the key? Which religion is the "right" religion? Which way of life is the "right" one? Is it right to have children? How many is the correct number? And if a woman has children, is it appropriate for her to think of other things? Can she have a career, or is she now obligated to think of nothing other than her children? How should a man treat his wife? How many wives should he have?

*The flawed premise "My group's/our way of life is the only correct way, therefore all other ways must be stopped, because when I look at what I do not agree with, I feel bad" is the basis of the majority of unhappiness on your planet.* <u>*Not only do those being pushed against feel the pain, but those doing the pushing feel it as well. In fact, the unhappiest, least fulfilled among you are those who are pushing against others, because, in doing so, you are disallowing the most important relationship of all: the relationship between you and You.*</u>

While it was your intention for new desires to be born within you and to accomplish those desires, you had no intention of hindering, in any way, the desires of others. You knew that this world is big enough for everyone to create their own desires. And you were not worried about being hindered by your observation of their creations (even if you did not like what you saw) because you knew you had the power to focus upon what is wanted. And so, ridding your world of your personal unwanted was not necessary. *You intended to decide what you want and, by the power of your focus and the* Law of Attraction, *to attract it—and to allow all others to do the same. You understood that diversity not only provides the basis of your strength and of your expansion, but of your very existence—because if there is not expansion, existence cannot continue to be.*

## Do We Have Power to Influence Others Rather Than Control Them?

**Jerry:** I'd like to talk more about the power of *influence,* or the power of *control,* we have over one another in our relationships. How much power over others do we actually have? And how can we avoid being influenced away from something that we want by another who thinks that we should want something different?

**Abraham:** It is good that you see that there is a distinction between *control* and *influence,* and we would like to take your understanding further still: When someone seeks control over another person, or over a situation, they never achieve it, because in the attitude of control there is such a big component of knowing what you *do not* want that your Vibration and point of attraction are working in opposition to your actual desire. *Even though you may join forces with others to push against the unwanted, and even when it appears that your forces have overwhelmed the opposing forces, you never actually gain control—but, instead, you enhance, or add to, your attraction of more unwanted. The faces and places may change, but more unwanted keeps coming, and you find no sustainable control.*

Also, there is little distinction between *seeking control of a situation* and *wanting to influence a situation to be something different than it is* other than the extent to which you are willing to go to try to achieve it. In other words, in the seeking of *influence,* you may use words to try to persuade—or even use threats of action to coerce—where in an actual attitude of *control,* you may offer stronger words or even take specific action to affect the behavior of another.

But there is an even more important distinction that we want to make here than the one between *influence* and *control,* and that is the distinction between trying to get to where you want to be from your awareness of what you *do not* want, as compared to getting to where you want to be from your awareness of what you *do* want. The first is more about trying to *motivate* another to a different behavior; the latter is more about *inspiring* another to a different behavior.

*In your effort at motivation, because you are focused upon what you __do not__ want, you do not have the benefit or help of your true power. But when you are focused completely upon what you __do__ want—thereby releasing all resistance or opposition to your own desire—you are engaging the Energy that creates worlds, and your power of influence is mighty. In your connection to, and allowance of, your true power, your influence to bring others into their own power is great.*

## How Do We Harmonize a Diverse Family?

**Jerry:** Regarding the family relationships between parents and children: How can an independently thinking, Leading Edge child who is learning and growing exist in harmony with parents who want to train him in their static way of thinking and behaving? In other words, what if your parents don't want to see change or new thought?

**Abraham:** This leads us to the explanation of yet another flawed premise:

> **Flawed Premise #5:** *Because I am older than you, I am wiser than you; and therefore you should allow me to guide you.*

While your parents, and others who arrived on your planet before you, do help to provide a platform of stability for you when you are born, they do not possess the wisdom that you are seeking. Your expansion will come from your personal experiences, and your knowledge will come from your Connection to your Broader Perspective. *Most of the guidance, rules, and laws that are passed down from generation to generation are written by people who are not in the state of "allowing" their Connection with their Broader knowledge. In other words, the majority of the guidance that is thrust upon you has come from a perspective of lack, and it cannot lead you to an improved situation.*

Of course there are things of a physical nature than you can learn from each other. There are many inventions and skills that have been discovered before your birth that you do not have to start from scratch in order to realize the benefit of. But there is a pervasive belief on your planet that is absolutely contradictory to *who-you-really-are* and to your reason for being, which leads us to the next flawed premise:

***Flawed Premise #6:*** *Who I am began the day I was born into my physical body. As an unworthy Being, I was born into a life of struggle in order to try to achieve greater worthiness.*

You did not begin on the day you were born into your physical body. You are Eternal Consciousness, with an Eternal history of becoming and of worthiness. And while a part of that worthy, Non-Physical, Eternal, *God Force,* Creative Consciousness expressed itself into the Being you know as you—the larger part of *You* remained, and remains, Non-Physically focused in Pure, Positive Energy and absolute worthiness.

You eagerly came into this physical time-space reality because it is the Leading Edge of creation and you are a creator. You adored the idea of focusing on this world of contrast because you understood the value the contrast would have in helping you, a creator, to focus and create. You understood that your own life would draw from you continual new ideas, and that, by the power of your focus, those ideas could become "reality," as it is known in the physical world. And you knew the joy of *choosing, focusing,* and *allowing* the creative manifestations. You knew that, in every moment, you would be able to feel the degree of Vibrational alignment you were achieving between your current thoughts and the understanding that the *Source* within you has on the same subject at the same time, and you understood that those feelings of positive and negative emotion would be the sole source of your guidance to help you create and discover and expand along your Eternal path of becoming.

You may remember how you felt as a child when someone focused their disapproval of you at you. The negative feeling you experienced was your indication that their opinion of you was out of alignment with *who-you-really-are* and what you really know. In that moment, you felt the beginning of the tugging of that other person pulling you away from your Broader Perspective of *who-you-are* with their distorted view of you. Your Guidance (the negative feeling) was letting you know that the focus that they had caused you to achieve was out of alignment with the focus of your *Source.* *While it never feels good to you to view yourself (or anything else) differently than the <u>Source</u> within you sees it, over time you became accustomed to the discomfort of your gradual disempowerment—until, eventually, you began looking to others for guidance, leaving your own Guidance to fade into the background.*

So now, getting back to your question of how a child can exist in harmony with parents who want to train him into *their* way of thinking . . . our dominant intent would be to, first, assist the child in remembering *who-he-is.* We want to remind him of his own *Guidance System;* we want to help him reconnect with his own personal power and realize his own personal dreams. But many would argue that it is just not as simple as that: "Even if the child were to remember all of that, he is still trapped in a relationship with people who don't remember, who don't agree with that, who are bigger than he is, and who are in control of his experience. How could a child ever find harmony under those conditions?"

First we will direct our response to the child in this situation, then to the parents, and finally to you who are asking the question:

### To the Child . . .

Your parents mean well. They are mostly just trying to prepare you for the struggles of life that *they* have found along *their* way. Their behavior indicates that they not only do not remember *who-you-are,* but they also do not remember *who-they-are.* That is why their behavior is guarded. They feel vulnerable, and they believe that you are vulnerable, too.

It would take quite a bit of explaining to your parents to help them remember; and if they were not asking, they would not hear anything that we have to say, anyway. . . . There is a good chance that you will be all grown up and out of their house before *they* ask, or listen, or remember.

If you are asking and listening (no matter how old you are), then we want to tell you the most important thing that anyone could ever tell you: *It does not matter what anyone else thinks about you. It only matters what you think. And if you are willing to let them think whatever they want to think—about anything, even about you—then you will be able to hold your thoughts steady with who-you-really-are; and you will, in time, feel good, no matter what.*

As you hear this and remember that it is true that *you are a powerful creator who wanted to experience contrast in order to help you decide the things that you now want,* it will help you to feel more patient about others' not remembering. When you remember that everything is responding to you and the way you feel, and you then gain control of how you are feeling, you will find tremendous cooperation from many different places helping you gain control of your own experience.

When you are alone and thinking about some of the trouble you have been in with your parents—you are inviting more incidents of being in trouble. But if, when you are alone, you are thinking about more pleasing things—you are not inviting more trouble. *You have much more control over the way others treat you than you sometimes realize. The less you think of trouble, the less of it you get. The less you think of your parents trying to control you, the less they try to control you. The more you think of things that please you, the better you will feel. The better you feel, the better things will go for you.*

It feels to you as if your parents are in charge of the way they treat you, but that is not true. *You* are in charge of the way your parents treat you; and as you hear this, and practice this, their change in behavior will be your evidence. And the best part is that you will be showing them (even if they do not realize it) how to enjoy harmony by *inspiring it* rather than *demanding it*.

### To the Parents . . .

*The more you see things in your child that you do not want to see— the more of that you will see. The behavior that you elicit from your child is more about you than it is about your child. This is actually true of all of your relationships, but since you think about your child more than most others, your opinion about your child plays a greater role in his behavior.*

If you could de-emphasize the unwanted behavior you see in your child by ignoring it—not replaying it over again in your mind, not speaking to others about it, and not worrying about it—you would not be a continuing contributor to the unwanted behavior.

When you hold anyone or anything as your object of attention, you are leaning in one of two directions: toward what *is* wanted, or toward what is *not* wanted. If you will practice leaning toward what *is* wanted when you think about your child, you will begin to see behavior patterns shifting to more of what you are wanting to see. *Your child is a powerful creator who wants to feel good and be of value. If you do not take score in the moment and decree him otherwise, he will rise to the goodness of his natural Being.*

When you are in a state of *fear, worry, anger,* or *frustration*—you will evoke *unwanted* behavior from your child.

When you are in a state of *love, appreciation, eagerness,* or *fun*—you will evoke *wanted* behavior from your child.

*Your child was not born to please you.*

*You were not born to please your parents.*

### To You Who Are Asking the Question . . .

Do not worry about a child losing freedom to unknowing parents, and do not worry about unknowing parents losing freedom to their children. Understand that all of them wanted the experience of co-creating in order to come to a new awareness of desire. Just see them all as having *Step One* (asking) experiences where they are continually clarifying what they want.

Through feeling parental domination, the *child* gives birth to desires about . . .

 . . . greater freedom.
 . . . being appreciated.
 . . . appreciating others more.
 . . . independence.
 . . . opportunities to expand.
 . . . opportunities to excel.

Through offering parental control, the *parent* gives birth to desires about . . .

 . . . having more freedom.
 . . . experiencing more cooperation.
 . . . the child having a good life.
 . . . the child being ready for the world he will step
        out into one day.
 . . . being understood.

In other words, this co-creative, contrasting experience is causing everyone involved to launch more rockets of desire and therefore to Vibrationally expand to those new places. And the only reason any of them ever feel negative emotion is because, in the moment of their negative emotion, they have not yet *allowed* the expansion. *Life caused them to become something that they are not currently allowing themselves to be; and both of them, parent <u>and</u> child, are using the other as their excuse for not being it. . . . Before your birth, you relished the idea of the contrasting relationships that would cause your expansion, and whenever you allow your own catching up with that expansion, you will then bless the seeming struggle that made it so.*

## Will the *Law of Attraction* Do Household Chores?

**Jerry:** Would you elaborate a little more on ways in which family members could *harmoniously* share in the responsibilities of common home maintenance and help with the general flow of the activities of the family, and still maintain their individual feeling of freedom.

**Abraham:** When you speak of *responsibilities,* you are usually speaking of *action,* and we certainly understand that there are plenty of action responsibilities to be shared in the making and managing and maintaining of a home environment. And we also understand how it seems logical to most people that when there are a specific number of things that need to be done and there are a specific number of people to share those tasks, an *action* regimen seems logical. The thing that usually goes wrong in such situations is that the people who are assigning the activities of the family are often doing so from a personal place of imbalance—not out of balance because of the amount of work that they are personally doing, but because of the resentment they feel about having to do more than what they feel is their fair share, or the frustration they feel about the work not being done the way they want it to be done. . . . *Even though we are talking about taking action to organize and maintain the home, it is still necessary to find personal alignment first. Which leads us to another flawed premise:*

*Flawed Premise #7: With enough effort,*
*or hard work, I can accomplish anything.*

When you are Vibrationally out of balance with your desired results, there is not enough action in the world to compensate. Without working to achieve Vibrational alignment with what you really want, but instead, offering action to push against, or fix, existing problems, the *Law of Attraction* will bring you a steady stream of problems to fix—and you will never get out ahead of them. If you are focused upon problems—the *Law of Attraction* will bring problems to you faster than you can fix them. If you are focused upon a disorganized home—the *Law of Attraction* will bring more experiences of disorder, disruption, and problems than you can keep up with.

*In simple terms, the power of the <u>Law of Attraction</u>'s response to your Vibration will always be stronger than your ability to keep up in terms of action. You just cannot get there from there. The only way to bring order to your life or your home—or your relationships—is to tap the powerful leverage of Energy alignment. And when you do, things that were formerly a struggle will seem to flow effortlessly.*

Unless you are able to let go of your chronic awareness of unfinished tasks and uncooperative family members, you will never be able to elicit good-feeling cooperation from others. You have to let go of the struggle, and focus upon the end result that you are seeking. *You have to find the <u>feeling-place</u> of a cooperative home that is organized and good-feeling before you can inspire that behavior from others. <u>The people in your life will always give you exactly what you expect. No exceptions.</u>*

Many people tell us that they believe that their negative expectations were born from observing negative behavior, and not the other way around. "I didn't *expect* my son to refuse to take out the garbage until he consistently refused to take out the garbage."

*You can find yourself in an endless loop where you explain that you feel negative because of the negative behavior of someone else. But if, instead, you take control of your own emotions and you think an improved thought because it feels better to do so, you will discover that no matter how the negative trend got started, <u>you</u> can turn it around. <u>You have no real control of what anyone else is doing with their Vibration (or with their actions, for that matter), but you have complete control over your own thoughts, Vibrations, emotions, and point of attraction.</u>*

### But What about When Our Interests No Longer Match?

**Jerry:** When people in a relationship that was once harmonious find that their interests have changed, and so now they are often in disagreement with one another, how can they find harmony when they have opposing beliefs or desires?

**Abraham:** This question brings us to another flawed premise:

*Flawed Premise #8: To be in harmony with another, we have to want and believe the same things.*

Often people are pushing so hard against so many things they do not want that they come to believe that when they find people who believe as they believe—who are willing to also push against those same unwanted things—in the joining of forces, they have found *harmony*. But the problem with that is, as they are focused upon what they do *not* want, they are neither in harmony with their own desires nor with the larger part of themselves (who is always in harmony with their desires). So their basic state of being, as they are pushing against their foes, is one of utter disharmony. And while they may find agreement with others who are also pushing against the same concept, or enemy, they could not be further from harmony.

*You must first find harmony between you and You, and then, and only then, is any other harmony possible. And when you consistently achieve harmony between you and You (which is what we refer to as the state of allowing), then it is possible to find harmony with others even though you have disagreements. In fact, that is the perfect environment for expansion and joy: diversity of beliefs and desires—but alignment with Source.*

Relationships are usually better in the beginning because you are both looking for things you want to see. And so, your expectation is usually more positive in the beginning of your relationship. Also, looking for positive aspects is a powerful tool in finding your own harmony, or alignment with Self. In the beginning, you both probably think that the wonderful way you feel is because of the harmony you have discovered with the other person, when what has actually happened is that you are using one another as your positive reason to find harmony with *who-you-really-are.*

*The Source within you only sees positive aspects in your partner, and whenever you are finding positive aspects, you are in alignment with* <u>*who-you-really-are.*</u>

### What If One Doesn't Want the Relationship to End?

**Jerry:** But what if your desires are *really* different from those of your mate? What if one of you has decided to bring your relationship to an end and the other wants it to continue?

**Abraham:** *We understand how that may seem like "different desires," but actually there is a powerful mutual desire at the heart of what both people want: the desire to feel better.* One believes that the action of separation is the most likely path to feeling better, while the other believes that staying together is the path.

Let us begin this discussion by pointing out another flawed premise, which is a big part of the basis of confusion on this issue:

*Flawed Premise #9: The path to my joy is through my action. When I am feeling bad, I can get to a better-feeling place by taking action. I can focus upon a situation that I think is the reason I am feeling bad, and walk away from it. And once away from it, I will feel better. I can get to what I want by leaving what I don't want.*

The positive moments you may have once felt within your relationship were not about the harmony you found with each other (that now seems to be gone), but instead about your own alignment with *who-you-really-are*. It is true that it is easier for you to be in alignment with yourself when you are not focused upon unwanted things. So a person near you who is pleasing to you *can* serve as a positive object of attention, causing no distraction from your alignment. But the belief that another person is "making" you happy is incorrect. *Your happiness is your natural state of being.* The correct understanding is that you are using this currently pleasant person as your reason *not* to focus yourself away from *who-you-really-are;* while, in your state of unhappiness, you may be using this currently unpleasant person as your reason *to* focus yourself away from *who-you-are.*

*Your true happiness happens when you discover that no one other than yourself is responsible for the way you feel. If you believe that others are responsible for the way you feel, you are in true bondage, because you cannot control how they behave or how they feel.*

It is natural that you would want to remove yourself from things that do not feel good, but in an inclusion-based Universe, that is not possible. You cannot focus upon unwanted things— and therefore activate the unwanted in your Vibration—and get away from it, because the pulling power of the *Law of Attraction* is stronger than any action that you may offer.

*As you walk away from one unpleasant situation, the <u>Law of Attraction</u> will bring another that feels very much like it, and usually quickly. You just cannot get there from there. To get to where you want to be—to that place of <u>feeling</u> better—you have to reach for alignment between you and You.*

## A 30-Minute Energy-Alignment Process

You can get a running start on a day of aligned Energy as you put yourself to bed the night before:

Find things in your immediate vicinity—such as your bed, your bed linens, and your pillow—to direct your appreciation toward. Then set your intention to sleep well and to awaken refreshed. When you find yourself awake in the morning, lie in more appreciation for at least five minutes, and then refresh yourself by bathing and eating. Then, sit for 15 minutes and quiet your mind. Feel whatever resistance you may have fall away, and feel your Vibration rise. Then open your eyes, and sit for five or ten minutes writing a list of things you appreciate about your life.

In doing this Energy-alignment work, your point of attraction will not only yield to you activities and rendezvous with good-feeling people, places, and things—but your ability to experience the delicious depth of them will be dramatically enhanced. Rather than doing things and going places to try to *make* yourself feel good, deliberately get to *feeling good*—and let those things and people and places come to you. It is possible that once you come into alignment with *who-you-really-are,* you will gravitate to a different relationship. But it is also likely that the relationship that you are already in was attracted from your point of being in alignment to begin with, and now that you have achieved alignment again, it will renew itself for you.

If you entered your current relationship from a place of mostly alignment, its potential for returning to a wonderful *feeling-place* is great. If you entered this relationship because you were in the process of escaping from something unpleasant, then the basis of this relationship may be more about what you *do not* want than about what you *do* want.

*In any case, getting yourself feeling good before you take any action is always the best process; and when you do not feel good, you cannot be inspired to any action that will solve the problem.*

## Is There One Perfect Person for Me?

**Jerry:** Is there the "one perfect person" for us to be in a relationship with? And if there is, do you have any recommendations of how to find that person? Also, what is your opinion about what we call a "Soul Mate"? In other words, is there an ideal Spiritual mate for each of us?

**Abraham:** Throughout your lifetime, and because of your interaction with others, you have been identifying the characteristics in others that are most appealing to you; and you have, incrementally, been sending out rockets of desires about those desirable traits. In other words, bit by bit, you have created (in your own Vibrational Reality) your version of the perfect mate for you. But before you can find your perfect mate, you must be a Vibrational Match to that desire, which means, you must consistently be a Vibrational Match to what you want.

If you are feeling lonely or frustrated about not yet meeting your mate, you are *not* a match to your Vibrational Reality, and so your rendezvous is postponed. When you are envious of others who have wonderful relationships, you are *not* a match to your Vibrational Reality, and so your rendezvous is postponed. *If you are remembering past unpleasing relationships and using those as your justification for wanting or needing a better one, you are a match to what you <u>do not</u> want, and what you <u>do</u> want is postponed. But if you can bring yourself to a place of consistently feeling good, even in the absence of the relationship that you desire, the rendezvous is certain. In fact, it is <u>Law.</u>*

The "perfection" of that partner means that your partner matches the things that your life has caused you to ask for, but the finding of that partner hinges upon you becoming a match to those desires first. You cannot find your perfect mate from your awareness that your mate is missing from your life. You have to find a way to no longer offer the Vibration of a "missing partner."

In the same way that from the sifting through your *now* physical experience, you are continually launching new desires—you also launched desires about your physical experience from your

Non-Physical vantage point before your birth. And sometimes those desires, or intentions, did include such specific things as creative traits or talents, specific things you wanted to do, or specific people you intended to co-create with. A "Soul Mate" would be such a person. But we usually downplay the idea of "Soul Mates" in the way that so many people want to address them because, really, *every person with whom you share your planet is a sort of soul mate.* And the feeling of Connection that people are looking for, the exhilaration of being with someone with their hearts soaring, really is not a function of the person you are with, but instead it is a function of your own Connection with You. We would prefer to think of *Soul Mate* as you mating, or consciously Connecting, with your own *Soul* or *Source* or *Inner Being* or *Self.* When you, in your physical moment and time, are offering a similar Vibration to that of your *Inner Being,* you have indeed found your *Soul Mate.* And if you *consistently* do that, the people who will gravitate to you will be enormously satisfying in nature.

*Think about what you want in a relationship and why you want it. Look for those around you who are experiencing good relationships, and feel appreciation for them. Make lists of the positive aspects of those you have spent time with. . . . In fact, one of the fastest ways to make your way to a wonderful relationship is to find any subject that consistently feels good, and focus on that even if it has nothing to do with relationships.*

When you remember that you have already Vibrationally created your perfect relationship, and that it is all queued up for you in your Vibrational Reality, and that your work now is to just not offer an opposing Vibration about it—and that it *has* to come to you—then it must come quickly. The number one thing that prevents people from rendezvousing immediately with their perfect mate is simply their awareness and discomfort about not yet finding one. Remind yourself, often, that you have done the work, you have clarified your desire, you have shot off the rockets of desire, Source is tending to those combined wishes, the *Law of Attraction* has organized the circumstances and events through which the rendezvous will occur, and now your work (your only work) is to stop doing that thing you do that *prevents* your meeting. When you are "doing that thing you do," you always, without exception, feel negative emotion. So when you are lonely, or ornery, or impatient, or discouraged, or jealous—you are delaying the meeting.

If we were standing in your physical shoes, we would remind ourselves that we have already done the work of specifying and asking. We would accept that the creation is already accomplished. It is done! And then we would think about it only for the sake of the pleasure of the thought. *When the moment of thought is blissful and satisfying—without the contradictory energy of trying to make something that has not yet happened, happen—your Vibration is pure and powerful, and your creation can easily flow without hindrance.*

### How Does One Find the Perfect Business Partner?

**Jerry:** If you were looking for a business partner, would you look for someone with exceptional ability and specific skills, or would you look for someone who is more compatible with your overall intentions?

**Abraham:** We want to answer your question fully, but first, you have led us to another widely believed flawed premise:

> **Flawed Premise #10:** *I cannot have everything that I desire, so I have to give up some things that are important to me in order to get others.*

If you have experienced relationships with others where there were some pleasing characteristics and some unpleasing characteristics, it is easy to understand why you would come to believe that you just have to take the bad with the good and put up with the unwanted parts in order to have access to the favorable parts. And since most people make very little effort to guide their thoughts beyond mere observation of *what-is,* they usually continue the pattern of focusing upon *what-is*—therefore getting more of what they are focusing upon—therefore focusing upon it—therefore getting more of what they are focusing upon . . . and then concluding that they have little or no control of those with whom they interact.

*By focusing upon the <u>wanted</u> characteristics of those around you, you train your Vibrational offering to match only the best in them—and then the <u>Law of Attraction</u> can no longer match you up with the worst in them. When you focus upon the worst of them, and train your Vibrational offering to match only the worst in them—the <u>Law of Attraction</u> can no longer match you up with the best of them.*

The people you would describe as having "exceptional ability" are usually those who are in alignment with *who-they-really-are. The brilliance or clarity or intuitiveness that denotes "exceptional ability" are also characteristics of a person in alignment.*

If we were seeking a partner of any kind, business or personal, we would first seek someone in alignment with him- or herself, because when people are tuned to the fullness of *who-they-really-are,* they are feeling good; they are inspired; they are a match to Well-Being, love, and all good things. . . . *The most significant thing that we could say about you finding such a person is that unless you yourself are in alignment, you would not be a Vibrational Match to such a person. . . .*

*Many people who are not in alignment then look to their partners to make things better, but the inherent flaw in that reasoning is that you do not have access to the aligned person you need to make it better for you if <u>you</u> are not in alignment. You just cannot get there from there.*

So our answer to this important question is: There are clearly happy people who do not have the skills or interest in your specific business, and there are people who may have all of those necessary skills required for your business who are not happy. *We would look for a talented person—with abilities that matched the needs of our business—who is obviously happy. In short, seek compatibility between you and You (which means, be happy), and then everything that you are looking for will find its way to you.*

## Who Is Best Qualified to Govern Us?

**Jerry:** In the area of government, who do you feel, among us, is the best qualified to set the standards, terms, and conditions of life for the rest of us?

**Abraham:** Your question leads us back to an earlier-mentioned flawed premise, that there are *right* ways to live and *wrong* ways to live, and therefore your objective as a society is to eventually find the right way to live and then to convince all others to agree or comply with this "right" way.

The diversity of your planet is of tremendous value and benefit because *from variety, springs all new ideas and expansion. Without the diversity, there would be complacency and endedness.*

Let us carry the flawed premise a bit further by pretending that your current population were to come into complete agreement with one another. Let us say that, by persuasion or coercion, you came to a worldwide consensus on the proper way to live. But new babies are being born every day from *their* powerful Non-Physical vantage points of understanding—and they are seeking diversity. It is such a perfect process where a small portion is coming into your environment (through birth) and a small portion is leaving (by death), while the largest part of your population remains, providing you with both continuity and stability.

*As individuals living life, you are individually, but also collectively, making constant Vibrational requests about an improved life upon your planet; and there is no possible way that you can individually or collectively cease the offering of these Vibrational requests—and the responsive Universe steadily responds to those requests.*

That stable central part of your population that we were just speaking of usually stubbornly holds to its limited beliefs (by attention to *what-is*), which prevents it from receiving the immediate benefit of the improvement it is seeking . . . but then the old, and therefore "more set in their ways," among you die; while the open and eager ones are born. *And so, life continues to improve in response to the asking that life summons from you.*

There are many who would argue that there are ideologies that are more conducive to a better life, and that even within those ideologies there are those who are better suited to lead and guide and make laws and decide what is the better approach to life, and all of that molding of the clay of your lives is pleasurable and satisfying. But there is something very much larger than that happening upon your planet: *You are billions of people, living the perfect diversity, just as you knew you would, constantly asking for improvement and thereby setting up, for the next generation, that improved life experience. If you understood that, and no longer clamored for the "one right way to live," things would go better for you sooner.*

So the answer to your question, "Who, among us, is the best qualified to set the standards, terms, and conditions of life for the rest of us?" is: *No one is more qualified than you to set the standards for you.* But there is nothing to worry about because you cannot cease making your requests, and Source never ceases answering them. And when you, right here, right now, no longer offer resistance to what you are asking for (by focusing on the opposite of it), it will reveal itself in your life experience immediately. In other words, if you focus upon something that your government, or someone in leadership, is doing that pleases you—then you are not resistant to the things you have chosen by the living of your life. But if you are bothered by something you see and are chronically pushing against it, you then use that unwanted thing as your reason to hold yourself in resistance to what you have chosen.

*Appreciate your government, or any other, in every way you can; and, in doing so, you will not disallow the thriving that is already set up for you, and by you, that is on its way to you. The powerful Law of Attraction always, no exceptions, is best qualified to deliver to you the standards that your own individual lives have set.*

### What Is the Perfect Form of Government?

**Jerry:** So, how would you envision the perfect form of government for us here?

**Abraham:** It would be a government that allows you freedom to be or do or have as you want. And that will come only when there is an understanding of *how* you are getting what you are getting. You see, your government, for the most part, has become one of rules and regulations primarily established to protect one of you from the other of you. *When you come to understand that you invite through thought, then you will not feel so much need for all of that restriction, and then your government can be established as it was begun—more to offer services rather than restriction or control.*

## What Is Our Natural Relationship with the Animals?

**Jerry:** How would you describe our natural relationship with the animals of our planet?

**Abraham:** The most important thing to remember about the animals with whom you share your planet is that they have come into this environment as extensions of Source Energy just as you have. In other words, like you, your animals also have an *Inner Being* or *Source* point of view; and, like humans, when their *physical* point of view varies from their *Source* point of view, they can also be in a state of resistance. However, the animals of your planet are less often in a state of resistance or separation. Unlike humans, they primarily remain in a state of Connection or alignment with their Broader Perspective.

When humans witness an animal who is tuned in to the Vibration of its Broader Perspective, they often comment about the "instinct" of the animal. What humans refer to as an animal's "instinct," we call an animal's "state of alignment with Broader Perspective."

Evidence of the alignment of the physical animal with its Broader Non-Physical counterpart is all around you, and so you accept it as animal behavior or "instinct," when what you are actually witnessing is a physical animal who, because it is offering no resistance, has full access to the Broader Perspective, and who understands, always, the larger picture.

## The Three-Step Process of Creation

In the Process of Creation there are three steps:

- **First:** *Ask.* (And the contrast of life experience causes you to do that.)

- **Second:** *Answer.* (That is not the work of you from your physical perspective, but, instead, the work of Non-Physical Source Energy.)

- **Third:** *Allow.* (You must find a way to be a Vibrational Match to what you are asking for or you will not allow it into your experience even though the answer is available for you.)

*When humans and animals come forth from Non-Physical, you come with different intentions.* Humans are more naturally involved in *Step One:* focusing, and sifting through the contrast of your time and space for the express purpose of *asking,* with ever-increasing clarity, for improved life experience. Animals are more naturally involved in *Step Three:* maintaining their alignment with their Broader Perspective. *Humans are here to specifically create through more specific focus. Animals do less specific creating and are much less inclined to sift through contrast and make decisions. In simple terms, humans are more creative, and animals are more allowing. That is your natural bent.*

While animals do experience contrast, and they do Vibrationally ask for improved conditions, they remain more often in alignment with their Broader Perspective than humans do. It is possible to be actively involved in sifting through contrast, as humans are, and to deliberately guide your thoughts into resonance with your Broader Perspective and experience the benefit of being an active creator at the same time that you are in the state of allowing. And while the animals of your planet are an important source of food for each other and for humans, the greatest value they bring to life on planet Earth is the Vibrational balance they provide, as they are extensions of *Source Energy* and remain predominantly in alignment with that Energy. *Humans and animals make a very nice combination, just as you knew you would.*

## Can We Influence Animals, or Only Control Them?

**Jerry:** Can humans *influence* the other living things on the planet, or do humans only have *control* over them? Like breaking or controlling a horse?

**Abraham:** *Control never proves to be satisfying for the one attempting the control or the one being controlled, because both—controlling others and being controlled by others—are unnatural to man and beast.*

With the absence of the offering of control, all would find alignment with *Source,* and all would experience harmonious co-creating with one another. Whether man or beast, you have inherent, innate selfish natures that you Eternally seek to satisfy. In other words, when you are in complete alignment with the Source within you, and therefore experiencing the benefit of that Broader Perspective, control of another is never necessary to your survival or Well-Being. In that state of alignment, you are always guided to circumstances that will accommodate the Well-Being that you seek. Only someone not in that state of alignment would ever seek control over another.

While in the state of alignment, you offer no Vibration contradictory to your intent; and when it is without contradiction, in that powerful state of alignment, the *Law of Attraction provides evidence of that nonresisted intention. That is what influence is: when you are in that state of Connection, your power of influence is very strong, because it is only your contradictory Vibration that ever causes you to be weak.*

Being in a state of powerful influence does not mean that you can get someone to stop doing what he intends to do and to begin pleasing you instead. It means that when you are not contradicting your own intentions—and are therefore offering a powerful Vibrational signal—the *Law of Attraction* will immediately bring to you people, circumstances, and events that match that signal. Everyone with whom you interact holds myriad intentions; and at the core of every one of them is a Being who is Pure, Positive Energy. And so, when you are in a state of alignment, you can then connect with the true nature of them. *Focusing upon your own alignment is the best way to maintain your power of influence.*

*Animals intuitively move toward anything or anyone who offers benefit, and away from anyone or anything who does not offer benefit.*

## What about Our Optimal Physical/Non-Physical Relationship?

**Jerry:** How would you describe the relationship between us current human Beings and *Non-Physical Intelligence?* And what would you describe as the optimal relationship between the two?

**Abraham:** This is a profoundly important question, and, in fact, is at the basis of this entire book on *relationships. The relationship between you and your Source is the most significant relationship of all, and unless this relationship is understood, all other relationships cannot be clearly understood.*

As you stand in your physical body, it is rather easy for you to perceive yourself as separate from others whom you can see. You make clear distinctions between "me" and "you" as you integrate your life with the lives of those who surround you. And, in a similar way, "mankind" has perceived what it calls *"God"* or *"Source"* or *"Non-Physical"* as separate, also.

*While focused into your physical body, you are an extension of that which is "Source," and the most important clarification of all here is that Source sees no separation at all between you, in your physical body, and Source.* Any separation, or disallowing of a complete integration or alignment between you in your physical body and the Source within you, is caused from your physical viewpoint and behavior, not the viewpoint or behavior of Source.

*Source,* or your *Inner Being*—or whatever you want to call that Non-Physical part of you—understands the Eternal relationship between the physical and Non-Physical aspects of you. *Source* also understands the Eternal relationship between you and every other physical Being with whom you share your planet, but we will discuss that more fully in other sections of this book.

So, here, in this book about *relationships,* we are asking you to reframe your definition of your relationship with Non-Physical Intelligence in this important way: Usually, when you think of a relationship between two people, you see them as separate individuals, or entities, who behave or interact with one another. We want you to understand that you are not separate from your Source, but an extension of your Source; and we want you to be aware of, or feel, your Vibrational alignment, or discord, with that Broader part of you at all times. We want you to be consciously aware when the thought you are thinking right now harmonizes so completely with your Broader Perspective that the full knowledge of your Broader Perspective flows through you, causing you to feel enlivened, clear-minded, and joyous. And when you feel confused or angry, or uncomfortable in any way, we want you to recognize that the thought you are thinking is discordant and out of harmony with your Broader Non-Physical viewpoint.

The relationship between "mankind" and "Non-Physical Intelligence" equals your *Guidance System.*

The relationship between "mankind" and "Non-Physical Intelligence" equals the expansion of *All-That-Is.*

The relationship between "mankind" and "Non-Physical Intelligence," from the viewpoint of *Source,* is that there is no separation, ever, between the two.

The relationship between "mankind" and "Non-Physical Intelligence," from your physical point of view, is a variable. The better you feel, the more complete the Connection or relationship. The worse you feel, the more fragmented the Connection or relationship.

Your question comes right to the heart of the intention of this book and the intention that "mankind" held when you came forth into your physical bodies: *You came as physical extensions of Source Energy, understanding that you would explore contrast, causing expansion not only for you but for <u>All-That-Is.</u> And you knew that, at all times, even while you were reaching into uncharted territories, the Guidance from within would not waver, but would remain a constant signal of Well-Being that you could reach toward and find at all times.*

*You knew that under all conditions, you could find your way back to the resources of your Source by "feeling" your way—by understanding that the relationship between you and You is not one of separateness but one of alignment and resonance. . . . When you master the <u>Art of Allowing</u> your consistent alignment with the Source within you—every other relationship will be beneficial and pleasurable.*

## What If One's Workplace Feels Uncomfortable?

**Jerry:** Abraham, if a person has a job that he enjoys, but he's being harassed by an oppressive, overbearing superior, would you recommend that he change jobs, or can you offer a better solution?

**Abraham:** This leads us to another flawed premise:

> **Flawed Premise #11:** *If I leave an unwanted situation,*
> *I will find what I am looking for.*

*Whatever you are giving your attention to is offering a Vibrational frequency, and your attention to it for an extended period of time causes that same frequency to be active within you.* It is important to remember that when a Vibration is active within you, taking the physical action of walking away from it will not prevent it from being present in your experience. In clearer terms, the *action* of walking away does not hold enough power to compensate for the *attraction power* of your thoughts.

By the time you come to the point of using strong labels such as *oppressive* or *overbearing* to describe someone you are working with, you have undoubtedly been observing unwanted conditions for some time, which means you have been practicing a pattern of thought and a pattern of resistant Vibration, and that means your point of attraction now is quite strong. So even if you take the physical steps to remove yourself from the situation by quitting your job and finding another—or by asking to be removed from the specific department of this supervisor and moving to another—*wherever you go, you will be taking yourself with you.*

Taking the action of walking away does not mean that your Vibrational patterns have changed; and, usually, even though someone may not now be observing the unwanted characteristics of his former superior, often he justifies the necessity of the move to the new location by continuing to remember or explain what the previous experience was like, therefore keeping that Vibration active within him.

You have received tremendous value in this *harassing, oppressive* relationship even though it is difficult to recognize it while it is happening, because during those uncomfortable moments when you knew so very clearly how you did *not* want to be treated, how you did *not* want your job to be, how you did *not* want to be devalued, how you did *not* want to be disrespected, how you did *not* want to be misunderstood—during those experiences, you were launching rockets of desire about what you *did* prefer and how you *did* want to be treated. In other words, those unpleasant experiences were the bouncing-off place for your expanded and improved life experience.

Every time something happened that caused you to launch one of those rockets of desire, the larger part of you—your *Source,* or *Inner Being*—followed the rocket, took the expansion, and held for you the position of the improved experience. The only open question, then, is: *Where are you in relationship to the expansion? Are you imagining the improvement, appreciating the contrast that caused it? Are you looking forward with optimism to the improved life experience regarding your work environment? Or are you continuing to speak of the injustices of your past experience and therefore holding yourself out of alignment with the new expansion that this relationship has spawned?*

Negative emotion means that your life has caused expansion, which, in the moment of the negative emotion, you are disallowing. Every time. No exceptions. That means that no matter what you believe is the cause of your negative emotion (and certainly we understand why you want to justify your negative feelings, because it *would* feel better if *they* would be nicer), *your negative emotion means that you are disallowing your own expansion.* Period.

If your harassing supervisor had not inspired your desire and expansion into something more, you would not suffer the discomfort of not allowing the expansion. So the better solution you are asking for is this: *Try to make peace with where you are,* perhaps by acknowledging that this unpleasant person has helped you become very clear about how you want to be treated and about how you want to treat others; look for the benefit of the relationship rather than pushing against the unwanted aspects of it; and, in the simple, and much-easier-than-you-may-at-first-believe, process of just chilling out a bit—and maybe even trying to give the benefit of the doubt to your supervisor—your resistance will subside and you will then be allowing yourself to move in the direction of your newfound expansion. . . . *If your life has caused you to ask for an improved situation—no matter what it is—and you are no longer offering chronic thought-Vibrations that are opposite of your desire, your desire must come to you. But you cannot continue to keep alive within you Vibrational patterns of what you do not want, and receive what you do want. That defies the* <u>*Law of Attraction.*</u>

### How Can We All "Have It All"?

**Jerry:** You said that we can have it *all,* but how does that work when there are others who are also wanting it *all?* What keeps our desires from clashing?

**Abraham:** There is a very large flawed premise that must be reconciled here before you will be able to understand our answer to your very important question:

*Flawed Premise #12: There is a finite container of resources that we are all dipping into with our requests. Therefore, when I satisfy my request for something, I deprive others of that resource. All of the abundance, resources, and solutions already exist, merely waiting to be discovered; and if someone else gets there first, then the rest of us will be deprived of that discovery.*

What many are regarding as the "discovery" of abundance or resources or solutions, we want you to understand is actually the "creation" of abundance, resources, and solutions. *When the living of your life causes you to desire an improvement—your Vibrational request for that improvement sets forth the process of the attraction and actualization of that improvement. In living your Leading Edge lives, you are not merely discovering improved benefits. You are creating them.*

Many people deprive themselves of much that they desire because of their misunderstanding of the ever-evolving, ever-expanding, ever-created pool of resources. If you do not understand the Creative Process of your planet, and the important role that you play in the expansion, you may fall into the ranks of the many who experience the shortage Consciousness that is caused by this misunderstanding.

This misunderstanding is at the heart of the feeling of competition. You did not come here to compete for the resources of your planet. You came as creators. *If your time-space reality has the wherewithal to inspire a desire within you, it is our absolute promise to you that your time-space reality has the ability to deliver, in full-manifested form, the reality of the desire it has inspired.* You came here knowing that; and until you remember it fully, and apply it deliberately, you will pinch yourself off from your largest of resources—the clarity, knowledge, and Energy of your *Source.* That is truly the only shortage that can exist in your world; and it is wonderful when you realize that that shortage is always, without exception, self-inflicted.

And so, you are not in competition with the others who share your planet. They could never deprive you of something by taking it for themselves. In fact, their existence *enhances* your ability to receive, for in your interaction with them, your own desires are inspired. *Any and all desires can be fulfilled unless you are holding yourself out of alignment with your own desire. The feeling of competition or shortage, or limitation of resources, means you are out of alignment with your own desire.*

### Are Legal Contracts Counterproductive to Creativity?

**Jerry:** I understand that you are encouraging us to be aware of our current emotions in order to make our best choices. So how can we live and create "in the moment" while, at the same time, entering into long-term relationships or agreements where our legal documents are often binding far into our future?

**Abraham:** Whether you are focused upon an immediate situation, which requires your thought and action right now, or whether you are thinking about a future or even a past event—you are doing it right now. Therefore, it is causing an activation of Vibration right now. In other words, you can tell how you are affecting a future event, right now, by the way you are feeling about it right now as you are thinking about it. Therefore, if you are aware of how you are feeling in every present moment, and it matters to you that you feel good, and so you are deliberately making an effort to align your current thought with the thought of your *Inner Being*—not only will you have many more pleasant moments, *but every subject that you have pondered will benefit by the focus of your Source-aligned thought.*

Sometimes people disagree with the premise that "if you feel really good about something, it will continue to evolve in a pleasing way," by pointing out how happy they felt at the beginning of a relationship that turned out badly. But if you remember that each time you focus upon something, your current thought is affecting it, then you may understand that between the time you felt good about your relationship and the time it turned out badly, your current thought moved often to what you did *not* want rather than to what you *did* want. Sometime, in the interim between the happy beginning and unhappy ending of your relationship, your thoughts turned consistently toward unwanted things, and you experienced the inevitable negative emotion that always accompanies such thoughts. *It requires continual deliberate focusing upon the positive aspects of any relationship to maintain the good-feeling productivity of it over time. You cannot allow your "now" thoughts to drift toward unwanted without having both current and future negative impact upon the object of your attention.*

Many long-term agreements are sought from a standpoint of wanting to protect against future unwanted situations, and that is not a good basis from which to begin any relationship. *When you come to understand the power of your focused thought, any need to protect will dissipate, and your sense of continual Well-Being will dominate.*

If your current circumstances, or the laws of your government, require that you enter into binding, long-term agreements, you can still maintain your balance and feeling of alignment, or freedom, by remembering that even those agreements can be changed. You may enter into a 20- or 30-year agreement regarding the purchase of your home, but later on, if you wish, you could sell your home and therefore end that agreement. Many people enter into "until death do us part" marriage relationship agreements, later to amend those agreements with new agreements of "divorce."

*It is liberating to realize that by utilizing the power of your thoughts— by deliberately aligning them with the expanded version of your life that you have given birth to—you can get anywhere you want to be from wherever you are.*

## What Perpetuates Chronic Therapeutic Problems?

**Jerry:** It seems to me that when people enter into therapy where they are trying to work out or fix specific problems, the problems often seem to continue for years. What's the cause of that? Why does their pain continue?

**Abraham:** Because every moment is new; and, under all conditions, the components of the moment are changing and different from every moment that has been before. *Nothing ever remains the same. Things are constantly changing, but often, because of chronic patterns of thoughts, even though things are changing—they are changing to more of the same.*

It is not possible to create an improved future by dwelling on the problems of the past. That simply defies *Law. Focusing on problems of the past, or the present, will prevent you from moving to the solutions in your future. Focusing on the problems of the past, or the present, will guarantee a problematic future.*

Therapy can be of value in the sense that any discussion about the unwanted aspects of your life experience can help you to know more clearly what changes you prefer, but beyond that discovery, *a continued discussion of unwanted things will only hold you in those unwanted patterns of attraction. If, however, once you are keenly aware of what you do prefer, you will focus upon that, your life must improve.*

There is a tremendous difference in the Vibrational frequency of the *problem* and that of the *solution*. The *question* is one Vibration, while the *answer* is something quite different. Your unwanted experience has launched an amended desire, and your *Inner Being* is now focused entirely upon that *improvement;* and when you join your *Inner Being* in the thought and Vibration of that desire, you will feel immediate improvement in your emotion—and the manifestation of the improvement will begin to move into your experience. But as long as you continue to beat the drum of injustice, unfairness, or that which is unwanted, you will hold yourself apart from the improvement.

## What Is Our Greatest Value to Those in Need?

**Jerry:** If we see a friend in a negative situation, living something truly unwanted or without something the person very much does want, how can we help? In other words, how can we be of an advantage to others rather than a disadvantage?

**Abraham:** Whether your friend is feeling negative emotion because of the situation he is in, or whether you are feeling negative emotion because of your awareness of the situation your friend is in, neither of you is aligned with your Broader Perspective. *Your awareness of your friend's problem is a true disadvantage to him, because you are amplifying the Vibration of the problem and therefore adding to it.*

Often your friend draws you into keener awareness of the problem by continually discussing specific aspects of it, but with every moment of attention that you give to your friend's problem, the further from really helping him you are.

In this contrasting world in which you are focused, any attention to your problems *does* cause you to Vibrationally ask for solutions, and those solutions *do* begin lining up for you. And so, you could actually add to the power with which your friend is asking for solutions by discussing the specifics of the problem, but he does not need help in amplifying his problems in order to intensify his asking. That is a natural process that the contrast of the Universe provides. . . . *There is no reason to deliberately stir up problems in order to stir up solutions.*

You are of no discernible assistance to your troubled friend unless you are able to focus in the direction of the solution, in the direction of what he wants, or in the direction of what you desire for him. *If you are determined to feel good and are able to focus in the direction of improvement for him despite his continual prodding at his problem, your power of influence toward improvement will be powerful.* In other words, when you focus in the direction of the solution, you join forces with your own *Inner Being,* with his *Inner Being,* and with all of the cooperative components that the *Law of Attraction* has already assembled. *If you allow yourself to be the sounding board for your friend's problems, your power of influence will be paltry, and you will be of no value to your friend.*

But something even more troubling is now occurring: Your friend's problem not only launched rockets of desire into *his* Vibrational Reality, but your association with him and your focus has caused you to launch rockets of desire about your friend into *your* Vibrational Reality. In other words, this experience has caused an expansion in you, and if you do not focus in the direction of your expansion—if you do not focus on the possible improvement for your friend—you will pull against your own expansion.

It is important to realize that the negative emotion that you often feel when you are worried about a troubled friend is actually present because your focus is pulling you apart from yourself. Your friend may be the reason for your focus, but your friend is not the reason you are pulling against yourself. Your focus is the reason for that.

*Looking for positive aspects and expecting good outcomes for your friends is the only way you can be of value to them, for there is no action that you can offer that is strong enough to buck your current of negative attention.*

**Jerry:** So we're not doing ourselves or the other person any favor when we discuss our problems or concerns with them?

**Abraham:** Indeed not. *Nothing good ever comes from focusing in opposition to what you desire. It is detrimental to you and to whomever you draw into your negative conversation.*

## Why Do Some People Repeatedly Attract Painful Relationships?

**Jerry:** What is it that causes some people to repeatedly attract relationships that bring them pain and anger—to the degree that they finally end the relationship—but then they soon find themselves engaged in another relationship with essentially the same sort of negative conditions? And what would you recommend to change that pattern?

**Abraham:** It is possible to walk away from an unwanted situation without repeating it again, but that would require not talking about it, not thinking about it, and not pushing against it. It would require a complete deactivation of the Vibration of the troubling experience. And the only way to deactivate a thought, or Vibration, is to activate another. *The way to avoid repeating <u>unwanted</u> situations is to talk about <u>wanted</u> situations. Talk about what you do want; and discontinue dialogue about any unwanted experiences, situations, or results.*

Monitoring thoughts can be tedious and tiring, so the best approach to deliberately change the direction of your thought is to reinforce your desire to feel good. *Once you are determined to improve the way you feel, you will begin to catch yourself in the more early, subtle stages of negative attraction. It is easier to release a negative thought in the beginning stages of it than after it has gained more momentum.*

## Are Some Doomed by Their Childhood Influence?

**Jerry:** Don't many of our disempowering thoughts begin in childhood? In other words, how much influence do adults have on the way children begin to think? And are children doomed to continue the patterns of resistant thoughts that they learn from their parents?

**Abraham:** *Doomed* is a stronger word than we would use, but there is no question that children are influenced by the thoughts of their parents, because anyone who is giving their attention to anything begins to offer a similar Vibration. But it is of value to remember that no matter what your age, there is always a Vibrational Relationship occurring between the Vibrational content of whatever you are focused upon in the moment and the point of view about the same subject from the Source within you.

For example, when an adult disapproves of the behavior of a child and speaks his condemnation of the child, as the child observes the adult's disapproval, a Vibration occurs within the child that corresponds with that disapproval. But, at the same time, the *Source* within is offering appreciation and approval of the child, because, no matter the situation, Source never withdraws love or offers condemnation. Ever! So the discord between the active Vibration, influenced by the physical adult's disapproval, and the active Vibration of the love of Source causes discord in the child, which feels like negative emotion. *When negative emotion is present, it always indicates discord between the perspective of Source and the perspective of you in your physical body.*

It is of value to note here that no negative emotion is present until opposing Vibrations have actually occurred. In other words, no matter how much disapproval another feels for you, unless you focus upon their disapproval long enough to activate it in your own Vibration—you will not feel the discord. But most parents are so certain they are right that they work quite hard at staying focused upon what they believe is wrong behavior until they do manage to influence enough attention to their object of disapproval that the discord begins within the child.

It is interesting to note the striking difference between the behavior or approach of your Source and most of your parents: Your Source, no matter how extreme the situation, will never withdraw its love and appreciation from you. There is no behavior that you could offer that would result in the withdrawal of the Love of Source—while, quite often, your physical parent, who has lost conscious Connection with Source, seemingly demands your attention to what he deems your failure or misconduct.

Notice how reluctant your children are, especially in the beginning, to admit their wrongdoing to you. It is their natural instinct to continue to feel good about themselves even when you are finding flaws or misbehavior.

From the moment that you are influenced to deviate from your awareness of your own value, the most powerful desire that flows forth from you is to reconnect with that awareness of your value. There is no greater driving force in the Universe than the force of Well-Being and self-value. So even if you are like most children who have been born into an environment where most adults have lost their conscious awareness of that Connection, whenever you catch a glimpse of it, it calls you. And you feel it. *There is no greater purpose of this book than to activate within you a conscious decision to seek alignment with the Source within you.*

Whenever others attempt to guide or influence your behavior by the offering of approval or disapproval . . . as you try to please them, you are diminishing your awareness of your own *Guidance System. If we were parents standing in your physical shoes, our dominant intent regarding our children would be to make them aware of their own <u>Guidance System</u> and to encourage them to utilize it always. For we understand that there is no amount of physical knowledge that we could convey that could begin to approach the magnitude of the value of their continual alignment with their Broader Perspective. In other words, the coaxing of anyone into pleasing you, from your physical perspective, and thereby ignoring their Broader Perspective of Source, is a sacrifice that we would never ask of anyone.*

### Are You Blessed with a Difficult Child?

Many children are able to hold to their Broader Perspective even amidst strong human influence. They are often labeled by their parents and teachers as "problematic" or "troubled" children. They are often deemed "stubborn" and "incapable of learning," but we want you to know that a determination to guide oneself, and follow one's personal guidance, is an inherent intention that all are born with. Many are coming into physical form with an even more powerful intention of remaining connected to their own Broader Perspective, and the physical people who surround them are finding them less easy to dissuade from their own determinations. That is a good thing.

Many people have been socialized, in the sense that they commonly seek the approval of others, and they often live very difficult lives because it is no simple task to determine which, of the influential people who surround them, they should bend to.

And many people who have spent many years making an effort to fit in, to not make trouble, and to find approval from others finally reach the point of recognizing the futility of it, because no matter how hard they try to please others, the list of those who are *not* pleased with them always remains longer than the list of those who *are* pleased. And who gets to decide what the right way of living is, anyway?

You are living in the wonderful time of Awakening. This is the time when more people will come into conscious realization of their own value. It is the time when fewer people will attempt the impossible task of pushing the unwanted far enough away that they will be left with only that which is wanted. It is the time when more people will come to the realization that what they have been long seeking is not a change in the behavior of others, or in the world outside of them—over which they have no control—but, instead, an understanding of their own Vibrational relationship with *Source,* over which they have complete control.

## How Can One Move from Disharmony to Harmony?

**Jerry:** If you were a child born into a disharmonious environ-ment—or even an employee finding yourself in an unpleasant work environment—how could you remain in such a situation and still maintain a positive personal life experience?

**Abraham:** The first thing we would encourage you to do is to lay low, so to speak. Try to be as inconspicuous as possible in your awareness of the disharmony. In fact, do your best to be unaware of the disharmony, because in actually being unaware of the dis-harmony, there will be no active Vibration of it present within you, and the *Law of Attraction* will then leave you out of any discordant rendezvous.

But if, instead, you *are* aware of the unpleasant occurrences—if you seek to quell the injustices by drawing attention to them—then you activate a Vibration within you that draws you closer into the unpleasant mix. If, from your point of view, you identify wrongdoing and you point it out, those participating in the behav-ior you believe is wrong will rise up larger and push back at you in an attempt to convince you that it is really your point of view that is wrong. Then you push back, and they push back, and the discord looms larger while both sides are deprived of any lasting solution.

All *contrast* causes an asking for improvement by all parties involved, but usually those involved are pushing so hard against someone else that they render themselves incapable of seeing the solution, even though it may be quite near.

*Seeing what you do not want until you can no longer stand it, and then leaving the situation and going somewhere else, does not bring a lasting solution, because the reason you left is the dominant Vibration within you, which means more scenarios like the one you just walked away from are making their way into your experience again.* In other words, you did not change your point of attraction by moving to a new location, to a new job, or to a new relationship.

*It may sound odd, but the fastest way to get to a new-and-improved situation is to make peace with your current situation. By making lists of the most positive aspects you can find about your current situation, you then release your resistance to the improvements that are waiting for you. But if you rail against the injustices of your current situation, you hold yourself in Vibrational alignment with what you do not want, and you cannot then move in the direction of improvement. It defies Law.*

Since a powerful desire for improvement is always born out of unpleasant situations, the larger part of you is already experiencing the benefit of the contrast you have lived, and you can—much more easily than many of you believe—begin, right now, to receive the benefit of that contrast. It may not be easy at first, but it really is as simple as making the best of where you are.

*In every particle of the Universe, there is that which is wanted—and the lack of it.* By making a decision to orient yourself to look for what is wanted, you will change your Vibrational patterns of resistance, and it will not be possible to remain in unwanted situations for long periods of time.

### Must a Negative Childhood Lead to a Negative Adulthood?

**Jerry:** So, a child could be negatively influenced by a parent, but that doesn't have to be a continuing influence through the adult life of the child, does it? In other words, that's an individual decision that can be made, at any time, by that child who is now an adult?

**Abraham:** It is clear, by the way you have worded your questions here, that you believe that the small child has little or no control in relationship to the older, bigger adult. And so, you are delaying your expectation of things getting better for this child until he becomes an adult and can gain control of his own life and make his own decisions.

As an adult reading this book, you are in a position where you can consciously make your Vibrational relationship with your *Inner Being* your highest priority by getting into the Vortex of Well-Being and positively controlling everything about your life experience. But there is another way of looking at this: As a child, even a child in a negative situation who seems to have little control of your own experience, you have a better relationship between the physical you and the Non-Physical You than most adults. In other words, for most, the Vibrational variance between your two Vibrational aspects is much less in the early days of your life than in the later years because you pick up and continue more and more resistant thoughts as you move through time. That is why most children are much happier than most adults even though they seemingly have far less control. And this book is written to help you reverse that process.

*We want you to understand that at any point when you make the decision to be consciously aware of the relationship between your Vibrational vantage points (which means, anytime you decide that how you feel is of utmost importance to you), you can come into alignment, you can access the Energy that creates worlds, you can fulfill your reason for being—and you can live happily ever after.*

But until you decide to focus your thoughts into alignment with the Source within you, you will not feel good. *A joyful life is not about gaining control of the factors that surround you. A joyful life is about coming into alignment with <u>who-you-are.</u> Joy is not about controlling other people or circumstances. Joy is about controlling your own Vibrational relationship between the physical you and the Non-Physical You. It is alignment with Source that is joy or love or success or satisfaction.*

## Blaming Past Suffering Magnifies Current Suffering

**Jerry:** There are a large number of adults who are experiencing trauma in their lives who believe that their parents are the root of their current problems. As long as they continue to blame their parents, won't they continue to experience problems?

**Abraham:** For adults to be able to use something from their distant past (such as from their childhood) as their reason for not feeling good in their present, it is necessary to keep that unpleasant thought alive and active in their Vibration. *Whether their unpleasant memory is about a parent, a sibling, a bully at school, or an angry teacher, it is only their continued thought about that relationship that would cause it to still be an issue years later.*

We would define a *belief* as a thought you continue to think. In other words, whatever you are focused upon, thinking about, speaking about, observing, remembering, or contemplating—whether it is about your past, present, or future—that thought-Vibration is active right now. And your emotions are giving you, in the moment, feedback of how that current active thought is blending with the perspective of your *Inner Being.* When your current thought is not resonating with what your *Inner Being* knows about the subject, your negative emotion indicates the disharmony. And often, because you are not aware of the existence of this *Emotional Guidance System,* and you do not realize that you could shift your focus and improve the way you feel, you continue your discordant thought, and you feel bad and blame the object of your attention.

You innately understand that you are supposed to feel good, and when you do not, you know something is wrong. And it is easy to understand how, under those conditions, you would blame whatever or whomever has your attention while the negative emotion is present.

So, over a longer period, each time that unpleasant memory surfaces and you feel the negative emotion but you make no effort to control your thought and focus into alignment with the perspective of your *Inner Being*—your Vibrational discord gets stronger. In other words, your negative beliefs about your earlier life not only get larger and gain momentum, but you continue to bring them forward and to use them as reasons for your current disconnection from Source.

Many feel the futility of trying to resolve those past conflicts because often the main characters in their past dramas are deceased, and even if they are still living somewhere on the planet, most feel that the likelihood of their recognizing their wrongdoing is small; and, anyway, they believe the damage is done. . . . During those traumatic or dramatic childhood moments of real or perceived mistreatment, they were influenced by the situation to focus themselves out of alignment with their *Source Energy,* and they did it often enough that they established a belief (a chronic pattern of thought) that held them out of alignment whenever they focused upon that misaligned thought.

What this blaming adult does not realize is that the relationship that is disharmonious here is the one between him, in his physical form right now, and his Broader, Pure, Positive Energy *Inner Being.* . . . *His suffering is not because of childhood mistreatment, over which he had no control. His suffering is about his current, in-this-moment misalignment between physical self and Non-Physical Source—over which he has complete control.*

*It can be so liberating to focus your thoughts and therefore train your beliefs into alignment with your own Source and power. And it is so debilitating to continue the flawed premise that "others need to be different before I can feel good."*

### When Does "Fixing Problems" Simply Increase Problems?

**Jerry:** I guess my tendency, in years gone by, was to try to fix the problems. I believed that if I could think about them enough, I could get them fixed. But then most of the problems just increased.

**Abraham:** *The only way to solve a problem is to look toward the solution. And, when you are looking in the direction of the solution, you always feel an improvement in your emotions. Looking back at the problem always feels worse.*

It is that old *flawed premise* again: "If I push hard enough against what I do not want, it will go away," when what really happens is that the more you push against it, the bigger it becomes and the more often it manifests in your experience.

It is helpful to remember that every subject is really two subjects: *what is wanted* and *the absence of what is wanted.* It often seems like a fine line between focusing upon the problem and focusing upon the solution, but that line is not a fine line at all, because the Vibrational frequencies of the problem and of the solution are vastly different. *The best way to identify which side of the equation you are focused upon is by paying attention to how you are feeling. Your emotions will always indicate whether you are focused in the direction of your Broader knowing and your solution, or in the opposite direction toward the problem.*

## Abraham, Speak to Us of Love

**Jerry:** *Love* is a predominant word in our culture. How do you see humankind, in general, in relation to the word *love?*

**Abraham:** Being in the state of *love* means being in the state of complete alignment with the Vibration of the Source within you. When you are in the state of love, there is no active Vibration of resistance within you. For example, if a parent were focused upon the absolute Well-Being of his child, that parent would be in complete harmony with the way the Source within him views the subject of his child, and therefore there would be no resistant Vibration present—and the parent would feel "love." But if a parent is focused upon what he considers to be the bad behavior of the child, or if a parent is worrying about something unwanted happening to the child, those thoughts are completely disharmonious with the way the Source within him views the subject of his child, and therefore there is resistance present within the parent's Vibration—and he would feel anger or worry.

So, in the same way that the "problem" and the "solution" are very different Vibrations, the subject of "love" can be discussed from the state of being aligned with *who-you-really-are,* or from the state of being out of alignment with *who-you-really-are.* A mother who shouts at her child, "Don't you know how much I love you!" from her place of trauma or worry or anger is doing so from her state of misalignment. And so, even though she is offering the word *love,* her Vibration could not be more opposite.

One of the most confusing things that children encounter as they begin to understand language is the dichotomy between the words their parents offer and the accompanying Vibration. It is of such value to a child when a parent expresses, with words, what he is actually *feeling.* And of even more value when the parent works to be in alignment with the truest of his feelings *(love)* before he expresses anything at all toward his child.

### When Is It Time to Quit Trying?

**Jerry:** Why do people often continue to cling to relationships that bring them pain?

**Abraham:** Often people believe that having a relationship, even if it is not a good-feeling one, is better than having no relationship at all. And so, they stay because it seems less painful to be angry than to be lonely, or to be continually aggravated than to be insecure.

**Jerry:** And what degree of discomfort or pain should a person reach before you would recommend seeking a separation from the negative relationship?

**Abraham:** Walking away from exposure to unpleasant or unwanted things does give you the relief of not being continually confronted with those things, and you may find it easier to find more pleasant thoughts and to be more often in alignment with your Broader Perspective. But while there is often temporary relief following an abrupt departure, if you have left without actually achieving Vibrational alignment with the Source within you, the relief does not last—and the next relationship you attract feels, often, very much like the last.

Of course, if someone is experiencing physical or even verbal abuse, we would encourage a physical separation as quickly as possible. However, just removing yourself from the current situation will not stop your feeling of abuse if you continue to think about it, resent it, and use it as your reason for leaving.

*You cannot continue to focus upon unpleasant thoughts without keeping the thoughts active within you and therefore holding yourself*

*out of alignment with the solutions and relationships that you really do
desire. In short, you just cannot get to where you want to be by pointing
at the evidence of that which is unwanted. It defies* Law.

Often people are surprised to discover that by physically remaining in a relationship (by not moving out) but at the same time
deliberately deactivating the *unwanted* aspects of their relationship
by activating more *wanted* aspects, their relationship improves so
much that they no longer want to leave. We are not suggesting
that, in all cases, it is possible to suddenly focus so positively that
you cause personality or behavior changes in those who live with
you—but we do know that nothing can come into your experience
unless it is active in your Vibration.

Many argue that unpleasant things would not be active in their
Vibration if other people had not behaved in a way that caused the
activation. And while we acknowledge that it is certainly easier
to feel good when you are around good-feeling people, *we would
never go so far as to say that the behavior of others is responsible for the
way you feel, because you have the power to focus, and therefore attract,
despite the behavior of others in your environment.*

If, every time you see something unwanted, you merely move
to a place where, for the moment, you do not see the unwanted
behavior, in time you will have yourself backed into an impossible
corner of complete isolation. But if, every time you see something
*unwanted,* you realize that, in the same moment, your awareness of
something *wanted* is keener—and you quickly turn your attention
in the direction of the newly emphasized *wanted*—everything in
your experience will continue to improve.

Instead of physically removing yourself from the unpleasant
relationship, and instead of asking your partner to behave differently so that you could feel better by merely observing, if you would
ride each new rocket of desire that is born out of the continual
conflicts, your physical Vibrational patterns of thoughts (or new
chronic beliefs) would be such that the *Law of Attraction* would have
to match you up with different experiences. . . . *It is always true
that whatever you are living always matches your chronic Vibrational
patterns, or beliefs. And it does not matter even if you have an excellent*

*excuse for your negative thoughts and negative emotions—they still equal*
*your point of attraction. What is manifesting on every subject in your*
*life is an indicator of the beliefs you hold and your chronic patterns of*
*thought.*

It is very empowering to discover that your patterns of thought
do not have to follow your current situation, and therefore your
current situation (on all subjects) can change. . . . We do not recommend taking the physical action of leaving a relationship without
deliberately coming into thought alignment with the new desires
that have been born out of your current relationship. And then—
whether you stay in this relationship or move on to another—you
can have exactly what you desire.

# PART II

# Mating, and the *Law of Attraction:* The Perfect Mate— Getting One, Being One, Attracting One

## Why Haven't I Yet Attracted My Mate?

**Jerry:** As humans, we seem to be driven toward the idea of coupling, or mating, even from rather early in our experience. You have called it "co-creation," but it seems that many people, or even most people, struggle with this subject of *mating*. Many worry about finding the right mate or worry that they may not find a mate at all, while many others are already involved, but in rather unpleasant relationships. So what would you say to the large mass of people who are single, who haven't found a mate (and want to), or to the large percentage of people who do currently have mates but who find their relationships unsatisfactory?

**Abraham:** You intended to interact and co-create with other humans when you made the decision to focus here in this physical time-space reality because you understood that all joyful motion forward requires a variety of viewpoints from which to expand. *You knew that by interacting with others, new ideas would be born from the mix; and you knew that as the new ideas or desires were hatched from these co-creative experiences, the potential for joy was a sure thing whenever you individually or collectively focused in the direction of those new ideas.*

When you want to be joyful and you remember that your joy is not dependent upon the behavior of others—and you consistently look for good-feeling subjects to use as your chronic point of focus—all desires on all subjects will be satisfied. But, from your place of not feeling good—as you worry about not finding a mate, or notice that you are unhappy with the one you have—your desire for a good relationship cannot come to you because you are not a Vibrational Match to your own desire.

Whether you are without a mate and trying to find one or unhappy with the mate you currently have, your work is the same: *you must find thoughts about your relationship that harmonize with the thoughts your <u>Inner Being</u> has about your relationship.*

If the strongest Vibration you are offering about relationships is about the *absence* of the relationship that you desire, then it is not possible for the *presence* of the relationship that you desire to come into your experience. The Vibrations are too far apart. You cannot find the *solution* to any problem when the *problem* is the most active Vibration within you.


### I'll Focus on What I *Want* in a Relationship

What it comes down to is, you must find a way of offering a Vibration that matches the relationship that you *want* instead of the relationship that you *have*. You have to ignore the *absence* of the relationship you are seeking, or ignore the *presence* of the unwanted relationship that you have, before you can get to the relationship that you want. And that is the tricky part. *You must make what you want a more dominant part of your Vibration than what you have; and once you are consistently doing that, what you want and what you have will intertwine, and you will be living your desire. In other words, until you have tended to the relationship between what you desire and the chronic thoughts you think—until you have tended to the relationship between the Non-Physical You and the physical you—no other relationship can be satisfying.*

When someone holds you as their object of attention and they are approving of, or appreciating, what they see, it feels very good to you because, in their appreciation of you, they are in alignment with their Broader Perspective. And as they hold you as their object of attention, you are flooded with the good-feeling Source Energy Perspective. But then if they look away, tending to something else, or lose their alignment by seeing a flaw or a fault, you may feel like the puppet whose strings have been dropped, no longer buoyed up by the behavior of another.

*While it does, and should, feel good to be appreciated by another person, if you are dependent upon their appreciation to feel good, you will not be able to consistently feel good, because no other person has the ability, or a responsibility, to hold you as their singular, positive object of attention. Your* <u>Inner Being,</u> *however, the Source within you, always holds you, with no exceptions, as a constant object of appreciation. So if you will tune your thoughts and actions to that consistent Vibration of Well-Being flowing forth from your* <u>Inner Being</u>—*you will thrive under any and all conditions.*

Most people, from an early age, develop an expectation that, at some point in their lives, they will find a mate. Whether male or female, they often hold a romantic image of walking off into the sunset, hand in hand. But they also often refer to that kind of relationship as "settling down," which indicates a somewhat negative expectation of giving up some freedom and some fun for the more serious experience of a permanent relationship. In fact, as they observe the majority of the relationships that surround them, they do not see those relationships as providing joy and satisfaction and freedom (which is at the very basis of *who-they-are* and what they want), but instead, they see *loss* of joy and satisfaction and freedom. And so, there is tremendous discord around the subject of mating, or permanent relationships, because while most people do come to expect that they will eventually mate with another, they often do not look forward to the loss of freedom they have also come to expect.

Sometimes people feel that they are not really "complete" until they find another person to share their life experience, but that is not a good basis for beginning a new relationship. It is another example of "you cannot get there from there." In other words, if you are feeling inadequate and are therefore looking for another to "complete" you, so to speak, the *Law of Attraction* must find another person who *also* feels inadequate. *Now, when two who are feeling inadequate come together, they do not suddenly begin to feel adequate. The basis of a really good relationship is two people who are already feeling very good about who they individually are. Then when they come together, they are a couple who feels good.*

Asking your relationship with any other to be the basis of buoying you up is never a good idea, because the *Law of Attraction* cannot bring to you something different from the way you feel. If you are consistently feeling bad about yourself or about your life and you enter into a relationship with another to make it better, it never gets better. *The Law of Attraction cannot bring you a well-balanced, happy person if you are not yourself already that. The Law of Attraction, no matter what you do or say, will bring to you those who predominantly match the person who you predominantly are. Everything that everyone desires is for one reason only: they believe they will feel better in the having of it. We just want you to understand that you must feel better before it can come to you.*

A woman, who was annoyed at our suggestion that she get happy and then look for a mate, said to us, "You want me to make myself happy by imagining my mate is here, even though he is not here. I don't think you care if he ever actually comes." She was right, in this sense: we knew that if she could consistently be happy, then not only would what she desires have to come about (it is *Law*), but she would be happy, in the meantime, along the way.

*It is amusing to us that people often seem to protest that happiness is a very big price to pay for successful outcomes. That is especially amusing to us because we know that the reason for every success they seek is because they believe they will be happier in the achievement of it.*

When you discover that your happiness is not depending upon outcomes of others, but that it is simply the result of your *deliberate* focus, you will finally find the freedom that is your most intense desire. And with that understanding will also come everything else you have ever wanted or will ever want. Control over the way you feel—over your response to things, over your response to others or your response to situations—is not only the key to your consistent happiness, but to everything you desire as well. *It really is worth practicing.*

*In simple terms, if you are not happy with yourself, or with your life, the attraction of a partner will only exaggerate the discord, because any action taken from a place of lack is always counterproductive.*

If you do not currently have a mate, you are in the perfect position of bringing yourself into alignment first, before attracting another person who will surely amplify the way you feel. But even if you are in the midst of a relationship that is often unpleasant, you can still begin moving toward a satisfying relationship anyway, because you really *can* get to wherever you want to be from wherever you are.

People are often eager to find their mate immediately, even though they are not currently feeling good about themselves. They even believe that finding a mate is the path to feeling better about themselves. However, the *Law of Attraction* cannot bring them someone who will appreciate them when they are not already appreciating themselves. It defies *Law.*

Therefore, if you are currently without the mate you want, it is much better to make peace with where you now are by beginning to accentuate any and all other positive things that are currently happening in your life right now, trying to soothe your discomfort about the absence of your wanted mate, making the very best of your life as it is, making lists of the good things, and coming into greater appreciation of yourself. It is our promise to you that as soon as you begin to really like yourself and you cease your incessant awareness of, and subsequent discomfort about, the absence of your mate, your mate will come. That, too, is *Law.*

If you are in the midst of an unpleasant relationship, you must find a way of distracting yourself from the negative aspects of the relationship. Some say it is more difficult to be alone and wanting a mate, while others complain that it is more difficult when you feel you are with the *wrong* mate, but we want you to understand that it really does not matter where you are currently standing or what you are currently experiencing.

*You can get to where you want to be from wherever you are—but you must stop spending so much time noticing and talking about what you do not like about where you are. Be a more selective sifter, and make lists of the positive things you are living. Look forward to where you want to be, and spend no time complaining about where you are. The responsive Universe makes no distinction between the thoughts you think about your current reality and the thoughts you think as you dream of your improved life. You are creating by virtue of what you are thinking about, and so there is no advantage whatsoever to pondering, or remembering, or observing, or speaking of things you do not want.* <u>*Make your active Vibration be about what you do want and notice how quickly your life changes to match your Vibration.*</u>

## Haven't You Observed Many Disharmonious Relationships?

**Jerry:** As a child, I remember observing many relationships, but I don't remember any that were happy ones. Most of those relationships were enduring relationships; they survived, but not in joy. I used to say that the majority of relationships I observed were experiencing a sort of "quiet desperation." I didn't hear a great deal of complaining, but I also didn't see much joy.

**Abraham:** Your childhood observation of predominantly joyless adults surrounding you is not uncommon even with children in your current time. It is much more common for children to observe their parents complaining about their relationships with employers, other drivers, the government, neighbors, and so on than it is for them to hear appreciation.

Most children do not have the advantage of observing parents who are in chronic states of appreciation and alignment, and so most children are developing unhealthy patterns of thoughts or beliefs about their relationships with others. But beneath those newly acquired unhealthy beliefs that they are picking up along their physical trail (as they observe the discontent of the adults who surround them) pulses a powerful desire for Connection, love, and harmony. In other words, even though, like you, children rarely see truly happy relationships, most are still hopeful that *they* will be able to find one.

We want you to understand that even if everyone you know is experiencing an unhappy relationship, there is a deep understanding within you that harmonious relationships are possible—and, in fact, every time something unpleasant occurs within a relationship, an equal desire is born out of it. . . . *The more unpleasant things you experience within relationships, the more specific your desire becomes about what you would prefer instead.*

The reason why the subject of relationships is such a big subject, and the reason why so many people feel overwhelmed by the prospect of improving their relationships, is because the more you experience what you *do not* want, the more you ask for what you *do* want, but your observation of what you *do not* want prevents you from moving toward what you *do* want. So you hold yourself, without knowing it, in the impossible tug-of-war of reaching for expansion while holding yourself back from the very expansion you seek.

There is one easy-to-achieve understanding that would put every relationship you have into alignment: *I can be happy regardless of what anyone else does. . . . By using my own personal ability to focus my thoughts, I can achieve Vibrational alignment with my Source (my Source of happiness), and I will feel good regardless of what others are doing.*

### But What If My Relationship Doesn't Last?

**Jerry:** I traveled a great deal in my life, and I was single a great deal of my life—so, as a result, I experienced a multitude of relationships. It seemed easy to begin them, but difficult to bring them to an end. And I notice that in our general culture as well, the going into a relationship seems to be fairly easy, but coming out of one is much more difficult. In the dissolution of relationships, in the settling of property, and so forth, there is often anger, violence, or revenge.

It seems like we observe so many relationships not working out and then really getting worse when they try to come to an end. Doesn't that also add to our guardedness or negative expectations regarding relationships?

**Abraham:** It seems, from the observations that you have offered here, that there are really no good reasons *to* enter into relationships. "If people stay together, often they are not happy; and when they attempt to end the relationships, things often really get bad." The most important thing that you are emphasizing with your questions is that most people enter into most relationships with negative beliefs about relationships; and those beliefs (or thoughts they continue to think) make it unlikely that their relationship will be a happy, successful one.

*While you have, deep within you, a desire for harmonious relationships, there is an even stronger, deeper tenet, or basis, of your very Beingness: your desire to be free. And at the basis of your desire to be free is your desire to feel good—and at the basis of your desire to feel good is an unhindered relationship between you and You.*

Whenever, for any reason, you feel less than good, you know something is wrong, and it is your natural instinct to identify the reason for the discord. Often you relate your not feeling good to another person who is present, or involved, while you are not feeling good. So then, as you do not feel good, and therefore are not in alignment, you believe that the person needs to do something different from what he or she is willing or may be able to do. And as you see that you are powerless to effect the change you believe is necessary, you do not feel free. So the most important desire at the very basis of *who-you-are* feels challenged, and your relationship breaks down.

But we want you to understand that it was a relationship that was based on a flawed premise to begin with, because it is never possible for another person to behave sufficiently, or consistently enough, to keep you in balance. That is your job. If you can accept, when you do not feel good, that it is no one else's responsibility to bring you back to feeling good, you will discover the freedom that is essential to your maintenance of personal joy. And if you do not, you just move from unsatisfying relationship to unsatisfying relationship.

*Your sense of <u>who-you-really-are</u> pulses so powerfully within you that you always continue to reach for satisfying relationships, because you understand, at very deep levels, the potential for joy contained in relationships with others. And once you decide that your happiness depends on the intentions, beliefs, or behaviors of no other, but only upon your own alignment—over which you have complete control—then your relationships will not only no longer be uncomfortable, but they will be deeply satisfying.*

In the absence of a personal Connection with Source, there is a feeling of insecurity that people often try to fill through their relationships with other people, but no other can sustain the Connection you need by giving you their attention. Many relationships feel good to you in the beginning stages because you are giving each other your undivided attention, but in time it is natural that your attention does begin to turn back to other aspects of your life; and if you were counting on the attention of the other, it is likely that, without his or her undivided attention, you will return to feelings of insecurity.

*A consistently good-feeling relationship occurs when each of the parties involved is maintaining his or her own Connection with Source. There is no substitute for that relationship. There just is not another person who can love you enough to compensate for your lack of alignment with Source.*

### Why Does the Relationship with Abraham Feel So Right?

**Jerry:** I know that there are many forms of, and reasons for, mating. There are marriages of convenience; arranged marriages; and marriages resulting from physical attraction or sexual lust, with high emotions exploding . . . and some people find mates because they just don't want to be alone.

But Abraham, I've been thinking about the absolutely perfect relationship that I have with you. Is it possible for those of us who are, right now, focused in our physical bodies to see others who are physical in the way I see you? In other words, can we get past the specific details, somehow, and get to the *essence* of a physical Being so that we can have the harmonious relationship with one another that I feel with you?

**Abraham:** You could not have asked a better question at this point in our conversation because what you are describing in your appreciation for what you are calling "Abraham" is the alignment between *you* and *You* that we have been talking about.

Your appreciation for us is not because we are behaving in pleasing ways for you, for there are many people who do not feel appreciation for, or alignment with, us. Some are not pleased with us when they realize that we will not *do* for them. (From their feeling of shortage or lack, they could plead for miracles or help from us that they would not find.) Others find us annoying because we are very clear about who we are and about what we want—and we are unyielding. We are not willing to set aside our intentions—which we have established over all that we have lived—to satisfy a whimsical desire of someone who is asking in this moment. We will not pretend that the *Laws of the Universe* do not exist as they do for the sake of entertaining you in this moment. And so, there are many who, as they interact with us, find negative aspects within us. And, as a result of their looking for and finding lack, our relationships are not satisfying.

The reason you feel that you have a perfect relationship with us is because you are currently focused upon the aspects of us that resonate with *who-you-really-are.* But you have the ability to hold anyone as your object of attention and do the same thing. It is *your* focus that is responsible for the way you feel about us, not something we are projecting to you.

When you are interacting with any others, it is always to your advantage to look for their positive aspects. By activating the Vibration of wanted things, more of those wanted things will flow into your experience. *When you discover the art of looking for, and finding, positive aspects in others—so much so that you develop an expectation for positive things from others—only positive things can come to you.*

**Jerry:** So, what I'm hearing from you is that the relationship I have with you, from my perspective, is a sort of self-love?

**Abraham:** Perfectly stated. By your appreciation of that which *we* are, you have come into alignment with *who-you-really-are.* And that is what love is: alignment with Source, alignment with self, alignment with love.

**Jerry:** So, in other words, from what I want in life, I have attracted you or am attracting from you that which fulfills me? And would you call that a form of codependency?

**Abraham:** *Dependency* indicates that "I am not whole, in and of myself," and that "I am needing another in order to be whole"; and that is not the case with you or with us. In fact, this question really points us toward a very important premise, or basis, for good relationships: When people feel insecure in their singularity, and so seek a companion to shore them up, the relationship is never stable, because it is on an unstable footing. But when two people who are independently secure and in alignment with their respective *Inner Being*s join together, now their relationship has a solid footing. In other words, they are not dependent upon each other for resources. They are getting those resources from Source, and now they can interact and co-create from that solid basis.

*When two or more minds come together that are positively focused upon a subject, those two minds are many times more powerful than one-plus-one. And so, the attraction of ideas and solutions goes beyond the sum total of the two individuals. It is truly exhilarating. And it is really what co-creating is all about.*

Something that is very basic to productive co-creating is that the individual creators who are coming together must be in a place of positive attraction before they come together, or nothing positive can come out of the co-creation. *If you are negatively focused and therefore not feeling good, you can only attract others who are in the same state of negative attraction. That is why looking for a mate from a place of insecurity, or lack of anything, can never bring you the mate you really want, but instead brings one who amplifies your current lack.*

People are often confused because they think their discomfort is about not having a mate. So then when they achieve the physical action of finding a mate, they do not understand why their discomfort does not subside or why it gets bigger. *The physical action of mating, or moving in together, or marriage, cannot fill the void that exists when you are Vibrationally out of alignment with <u>who-you-really-are.</u> But if you have tended to that alignment first, then the physical action of co-creating can be sublime. In other words, do not take the action in order to fix misalignment. Fix misalignment and then find a mate.*

## Shouldn't a *Soul Mate*'s Mind Be Beautiful?

**Jerry:** I hear people refer to "Soul Mates." When two people who are very positive in their thought attract one another, is that a form of what people call *Soul Mating?*

**Abraham:** Often when people speak of finding their Soul Mate, they infer that there is one specific person that they are meant to be with—a sort of soul alliance that they formed before they came forth into this physical body in this time-space reality. And while it is true that you do have intentions to rendezvous with others for the purpose of specific co-creating (and rediscovering those relationships can be tremendously satisfying), you were not looking to those physical rendezvous as the source of your alignment. Instead, you intended to accomplish a consistent alignment first, understanding that then you could attract those relationships into your life.

You could be in the presence of a person with whom you had a Non-Physical alliance, and if you were disconnected from your Source, you would not recognize the relationship. Often the people with whom you feel the greatest annoyance or disharmony are actually your Soul Mates, but, in your lack of alignment with *who-you-really-are,* you do not recognize them.

The best way to approach the idea of a Soul Mate is to seek alignment with the pure, positive Vibration of the Soul, or Source, within you; and then, by the allowing of that alignment, you will recognize every opportunity for these wonderful rendezvous, just as you have intended. The simple intention to find things to appreciate would put you in continual alignment with your Source and in the perfect position to attract your Soul Mates on myriad subjects.

Remember that even though you are new to this physical body, you are actually a very old Being who has experienced a tremendous number of life experiences, and through the living of all of that life, you have come to powerful conclusions. Your *Inner Being* now stands in the knowledge of all of those conclusions; and through your alignment with your *Inner Being*, you, too, have access to that knowledge—and anything less than that is out of balance and will not feel good to you.

### Nothing Is More Important Than Feeling Good

**Jerry:** And so, what would you say to young people who are just out of school, beginning their lives, seeking their first mate or between mates? How would you guide them regarding their relationships?

**Abraham:**

— First, we would remind them that nothing is more important than that they feel good, because unless they feel good, they are not in alignment with all that they have become, and anything less than that alignment will always feel lacking.

— Next we would encourage the continual setting of an intention to find good-feeling subjects to focus upon, and if a not-good-feeling subject should be activated within them for any reason, to do their best to distract themselves from that by looking for relief by focusing upon a better-feeling subject.

- For example, let us say that you observe an unpleasant relationship in progress, and you hear the negative conversation of this unhappy couple. Your desire for harmony, and even your more specific desire for a harmonious relationship, causes your involvement (by your listening) in this unpleasant experience. The negative emotion that you would be feeling is your *indicator* that this focus is not helpful to you. If you have in place an active intention to feel good, you would easily move yourself out of earshot of this conversation. You would deliberately turn your attention to other, good-feeling objects of attention.

— We would remind them that creating occurs from the inside out. *In other words, the thoughts you think and the way you feel are at the center of what you attract. Rather than looking for things outside of you that cause you to feel better, it is much easier to decide to feel better first and then attract, from the outside, things that do.*

— We would encourage a time of focusing upon what is wanted before jumping into any action. *When you take action as you focus upon what you do not want, you only get more of what you do not want. But if you take the time to focus upon what you do want before you take the action, then the action that is inspired will enhance your desire.*

— We would also advise them:

- As you move through your day into the variety of changing segments that make it up, stop often and restate to yourself your intention to feel good and to stay in alignment with your *Inner Being* or Source.

- Let your desire to feel good be the dominant intention that is present no matter what else is occurring in that segment. And remind yourself, often, that it is up to *you* to make that Connection and to feel good, and that no other person has a responsibility or the ability to make that important Connection for you.

- Look to your relationships with others as a way of enhancing the alignment you have already achieved, but not as a means of accomplishing the alignment.

- Independently, by your own focus with Source, reach the consistent place of loving yourself. Do not ask others to love you first. They cannot.

*The dominance of your thoughts is what brings everything to you and is what is behind the action that you offer. By seeking good-feeling thoughts that align you with your Source—your action will then always feel good. You cannot muster enough action to compensate for misaligned thought, but action that is inspired from aligned thought is always pleasurable action.*

### She Wants Someone, but Not *That* One

**Jerry:** Okay, so what would you say about a woman who seems to feel good about herself, who continues to express her desire for a mate, but who disqualifies them, one by one, as the parade of men moves through her experience?

**Abraham:** Her *desire* for a mate keeps the men coming, but her *belief* in bad relationships causes her to push them away. And her attention to unwanted characteristics makes it impossible for the characteristics that she desires to come to her.

If she is continually focusing upon what she does not like in the men coming to her, her chronic attention to the lack in others is keeping her from being in alignment with *who-she-really-is.* And under those conditions, she cannot be feeling good about herself or about anyone.

Finding lack in others is not the path to liking what you see in yourself. *If you are a person who has trained yourself to look for positive aspects, you will find them in yourself as well as in others. If you are a person who has trained yourself to look for negative aspects, you will find them in yourself as well as in others. Therefore, it is always accurate to say that no one who is critical of others really likes themselves. It defies* <u>*Law.*</u> *Whenever you see those who are very critical of others, you are actually seeing people who do not like themselves.*

The appearance of a superior attitude you sometimes see, which causes you to think that people really like themselves, is often their way of covering up the insecurity or lack of alignment they are feeling. *When you really like yourself, you are in harmony with the Source within you; and when that is the case, your appreciation of others flows abundantly—and when that is the case, wonderful things flow steadily to you.*

When you are in alignment with your Source, the *Law of Attraction* can then only match you up with others who are also in alignment with their Source, and the ensuing relationship is then one of satisfaction and delight. But when you are out of alignment and feeling bad, the *Law of Attraction* then can only match you up with others who also feel bad, and those relationships are unpleasant and uncomfortable.

You want to co-create with one another, but if you are not tending to your own personal alignment, then co-creating with others only exaggerates your misalignment. Interacting with others adds immeasurably to the expansion of your planet and to *All-That-Is,* and yet, most people deny themselves the pleasure of co-creating because of their attention to the unwanted aspects of those around them. In other words, for the most part, you are focused upon the worst in one another rather than the best of one another. And the reason for that is, you have not found your centered place before you came together, and so when you come together, you perpetuate the imbalance in one another.

### Relationships, and the *List-of-Positive-Aspects Process*

*Whether you are currently without the relationship that you desire or in the middle of a relationship that does not please you, there is nothing that you could do that would be of greater value in moving you in the direction of the relationship that you want than to take a notebook and spend time every day writing the positive aspects of the people in your life.*

Make lists of positive aspects about the people around you, the people from your past, and yourself. And, in a very short period of time, you can demonstrate to yourself the power of your aligned thought and the cooperative nature of the *Law of Attraction.* By releasing all effort toward the futile control of the behavior of others and, instead, focusing the power of your positive thoughts, you will find the delicious relationships that you have been dreaming about.

<u>*You are the thinking, vibrating attractor of your experience; and the thoughts you think determine everything about the life that you live. As you turn your attention toward the positive aspects of the personalities and behaviors of others with whom you share your planet, you will train your point of attraction in the direction of only what you desire.*</u>

The relationships that you desire are not only possible, not merely probable—they are certain. But you must train the frequency of your thought-Vibration into alignment with those desired relationships if you are to experience them in the tactile, physical, "real life" ways that you desire. *Not only does the power of your thought determine which people make their way into your life, but the power of your thought determines how they behave once they get there.*

### By Virtue of My Vibration, I'm Attracting

**Jerry:** In my early experience, I remember observing a common pattern where it seemed like most people were not interested in having a relationship with the people who wanted to have a relationship with them. It seemed like every boy was interested in a girl who didn't want him, and every girl wanted to be with a boy who didn't want to be with her.

**Abraham:** Well, the best part about your observation is that the contrast of their experiences was helping them to more clearly identify what it was that they each did want. This rather common scenario occurs because most people believe that in their search for the "perfect mate," they must root out the imperfections. They believe that by identifying what they do not want, and then by keeping a list of those unwanted characteristics, if they sort long enough, they will arrive at their desired destination of the "perfect mate." But the *Law of Attraction* does not allow that.

When the list of what you do not want in a mate is the dominant Vibration that you are offering regarding mating, the *Law of Attraction* will bring you a continuing string of unwanted partners. It is necessary to use your own self-discipline in directing your thoughts to the positive aspects of your current relationships before more of what you do want can come to you.

Over time, through your interaction with a variety of relationships, you have certainly identified many characteristics that you do not want in a partner. And each time your experience has helped you to identify what you do not want, you have been emitting a Vibrational request for what you prefer instead. As a result of all of those relationships, both those you have personally lived and even those that you have observed that others are living, you have created a Vibrational version of your "perfect mate." And if you could then give your undivided attention to *that* version, the *Law of Attraction* would bring to you only those who match that version. But if you continue to focus on the flaws or unwanted characteristics of those people, you will hold yourself apart from what you really want.

When we explain that the fastest way to get to the relationship you really want is by finding appreciation right where you stand (you may be in a temporary relationship, or you may be currently without any relationship), people often resist because they believe that if they say nice things about where they are, somehow they will get stuck right where they are. But that is not how it works.

When you look for, and find, positive aspects in your current situation, you are actually using your current situation as your reason to be a Vibrational Match to your own Vibrational Escrow, to *who-you-really-are,* to your *Inner Being,* and to everything you really desire. Feeling good about where you are is the fastest path to even greater improvement. But when you find fault with what is going on in your current life experience, the negative emotion you feel is your indication that your current thought and current Vibration is holding you apart from your own Vibrational Escrow, from *who-you-really-are,* from your *Inner Being,* and from everything you really desire.

*The reason why "the grass always looks greener on the other side of the fence" is because many people have developed very strong tendencies toward complaining about what is on their "side of the fence."*

## But What about When Others Choose Our Mates for Us?

**Jerry:** I'd also like to hear your comments on the cultural aspects of mating. There are many cultures where the parents, or the adults in the communities, choose the mates for their children; whereas, in our culture, we believe more in romantic love, where we fall in love with someone and choose our mates because we have fallen in love with them.

**Abraham:** Of course, it feels better to you, and therefore feels right to you, for you to be the one to choose your mate—or anything else, for that matter. But even in your culture or society, where you believe that you are freer to choose your mates, you are still very much bound by the beliefs of those who surround you. In other words, there are many within your freer-seeming culture who would not dare to marry outside of the wishes of their parents, religion, or culture. But we do agree that your society does allow more leeway than some others.

But there is an even more important thing we would like you to consider regarding the "choosing" of a mate. You are not making your choices with your words, but instead, with your Vibrational offering. And so, sometimes, without realizing it, you are actually "choosing" the exact opposite of what you really want. For example, people "choose" cancer—not because they want to experience the disease of cancer, but because they "choose" to give their attention to resistant thoughts that disallow the Well-Being that would be there otherwise. And so, in a similar way, people choose unpleasant partners because of their chronic attention to what they *do not* want, or their chronic attention to the absence of what they *do* want. In other words, a person who often feels lonely is a person "choosing" the absence of something very much wanted.

### Finding, Evoking, or Being the Perfect Mate

**Jerry:** So how would you recommend that someone find the "perfect mate"?

**Abraham:** In order to *find* what you are calling the "perfect mate," you must first *be* the perfect mate. In other words, you must consistently emit a Vibrational signal that matches the mate you desire. The not-so-perfect relationships that you have observed, or lived, have given you wonderful opportunities to decide and fine-tune the kind of relationship you would like to have. And so, you have only to think about those *wanted* characteristics of a relationship in order to train your own Vibration into one that matches your desire.

When you point out what you do not like in relationships, or remember unpleasant events from past relationships, or even watch movies where people are mistreating one another, you are unwittingly training your Vibration away from your *desired* relationship. And you simply cannot get there from there.

*You cannot get the relationship of your dreams when your chronic thoughts about relationships feel lonely or angry or worried or disappointed. But as you look for things you appreciate in yourself and others—as you make lists of positive aspects of past and present relationships—you train your Vibrational offering to match the Vibration of your desires, and your "perfect mate" must then come. It is* <u>Law.</u>

### *Wanting* a Mate, or *Needing* a Mate

[The following are examples of audience members' questions at an Abraham-Hicks workshop.]

**Questioner:** So it seems like my wanting someone pushes them away, but my not wanting them brings them to me. Why does that happen?

**Abraham:** When you *want* someone but the dominant thought within you is about the *lack* of that person—then your most active Vibration holds him or her away from you. When you do not want someone, but the dominant thought within you is about this unwanted person pursuing you—then he or she is drawn closer to you, by you. . . . *You are getting the essence of what you are thinking about, whether you want it or not.*

**Questioner:** Is this similar to the distinction between *wanting* and *needing?*

**Abraham:** Yes, and that is a good way of thinking about this. When you *want* something and are thinking about how wonderful it will be to have it, your current emotion feels good because your current thought is a Vibrational Match to your true desire. But when you *want* something but are currently thinking about not having it, about the absence or lack of it, your current emotion feels bad because your current thought is a Vibrational mismatch to your true desire.

The difference between *wanting* and *needing* is not just speaking different words. A pure state of *desire* or *wanting* always feels good because you are a Vibrational Match to what is in your own Vibrational Reality. A state of *need* always feels bad because you are a Vibrational Match to the absence of your desire and are therefore a mismatch to your Vibrational Reality.

## Is There a Way of Staying Positive Around "Lackful" Others?

**Questioner:** How can I remain positively focused when my mate is predominantly focused on lack and makes no effort to be positive? And it gets to me—it's hard not to also feel lack.

**Abraham:** We know that it is easier to feel good when you are seeing or hearing something that causes you to feel good, but it is extremely liberating to show yourself that you have the ability to feel good in any situation even when those close to you do not.

You will discover that it is far easier to learn to direct your own mind than to arrange, through action, the people with whom you spend your time. Even if there is only one person who is with you often whom you need to train, you could not train him or her sufficiently. And, of course, there are many more persons than one to whom you are having an emotional response. *When you do become adept at directing your thoughts to things that are pleasing, the unpleasing people (or unpleasing aspects of those people) will leave your experience. It is your attention to the unwanted that holds it in your experience.*

Many people disagree about that when they first hear it, because they believe that negative things are in their lives because someone else is putting them there: "My abusive husband asserts himself negatively into my experience." But we want you to understand that if you use your power of focus to withdraw your attention from the negativity or abuse, and put your attention upon positive aspects, instead—the abuse cannot remain in your experience. *It is empowering to discover that any and all negative aspects stay in your experience only because of your attention to, and therefore continuing invitation of, them.*

We acknowledge that holding positive thoughts in the midst of negative conditions is not easy. Especially in the beginning. The best time to begin to make the effort to direct your thoughts really is not when you are the middle of a negative situation. It will be easier for you to reach for better-feeling thoughts when you are alone: *Begin by trying to remember when you did easily feel good about this person. And if you cannot find that beginning place, then choose another topic altogether. The first thing that is necessary to break a negative trend and start it in a more positive direction is the acceptance that your thoughts do create the reality that you live. Next you must accept that you do have the power to direct your own thoughts. And then, what is required is a willingness to direct your thoughts in the direction of what feels better until that pattern is established within you.*

*One of the most exciting things about beginning the process of deliberately focused thought is that the* Law of Attraction *will bring you evidence of your improved thought immediately. And while old patterns may be hard to break, and you may slip back into those old patterns from time to time, the evidence of your effort will be undeniable to you. And,* before long—with much less effort than you spend trying to dodge negative conversations, or train another into better behavior—all of your relationships will improve.

### A Brief Bedtime Exercise That Transforms Relationships

As you lie in your bed before sleeping, if you will think of good-feeling things from your past or present, or even speculate into your future, you will set the tone of the Vibration in which you will awaken in the morning. In the morning, when you first return to Consciousness, try to remember what you were thinking about in the evening, and make an effort to reestablish that positive trend of thought. This one small exercise will change the way everyone you meet responds to you in this new day. And as you do that—night after night, and then morning after morning—new patterns will emerge, and your relationships will transform.

## What Am I Expecting from a Relationship?

You have the power to evoke from others the relationships that you desire. But you cannot get to a new-and-improved situation by giving your attention to the current situation. The Universe, and all physical and Non-Physical players in it, is responding to the Vibrations that you are offering; and there is no distinction made between the Vibrations that you offer as you *observe,* and the Vibrations that you offer as you *imagine. . . . If you will simply imagine your life as you want it to be, all cooperative components will be summoned. And even more important, all components that are summoned will cooperate. It is Law.*

You have the power to evoke from others a relationship that is in harmony with the freedom, and the growth, and the joy that you seek, because within each of the others are those probabilities. Within each of them is the probability of someone being very understanding—or not. Of someone being very pleasant—or not. Of someone being very open-minded—or not. Of someone being very positive—or negative. *The experience that you have with others is about what you evoke from them.*

Have you had the experience of behaving with someone in a way that you had not intended? It just sort of came out of you suddenly. That was you experiencing the power of influence from another's *expectation.* Have you noticed the personality of a child changing depending on which adult it is interacting with? Cooperative and pleasant with one person, and obstinate and cranky with another? You were witnessing the power of influence from another's *expectation.*

When you train yourself into steady alignment with your own Broader Perspective, you will tap into the Energy that creates worlds, and you will be pleased by the positive response that you receive from those around you. No longer blame others with whom you share relationships; and instead, acknowledge that you are the attractor of your experience. True freedom comes from that understanding.

As you tend to your relationship between you (in your physical focus) and the Broader Perspective of your *Inner Being,* as you train yourself into the good-feeling thoughts of your Source, as you come into alignment with *who-you-really-are,* as you learn to love yourself—the others with whom you interact will not be able to buck that current of Well-Being. They will either love you back—or they will gravitate out of your experience.

### What Are the Desired Characteristics of a Perfect Mate?

**Jerry:** Is it possible for one person, the same mate, to continue to be our perfect mate even though we are growing and changing and evolving? I mean, there was a time in my life when I was an acrobat, and I had to be able to throw my partner high and catch her, and so she had to be under five feet tall and weigh under 98 pounds. And when I met Esther, many years later, none of that was relevant anymore. Other things attracted me to Esther. And so, she was the perfect mate at the time she came into my life. So it seems like monogamy, or being with one person forever, could be pretty challenging.

**Abraham:** As you are moving through the details of your life experience, you are continually generating new preferences from the details of your new, current experiences. That process never stops. Those rockets of desire are received and held by your *Inner Being,* in your Vibrational Reality. In other words, every new experience causes you to amend, in small and large ways, your new version of the life you desire; and your *Inner Being* never ceases to keep up with the new version.

As you, through the power of your focus, hold yourself predominantly in an attitude of feeling good, you stay up to speed with your own Vibrational Reality, and so it continues to unfold and present itself to you in natural and comfortable ways. In other words, you have a continuing feeling of *This is the next logical step* as you *allow* the perfect unfolding of your own life experience. And so, it is possible that a new partner is "the next logical step" for who you have become, but if that is the case, the releasing of one mate and the receiving of another would not be an uncomfortable or unpleasant situation.

It is a rather illogical and impossible standard that your culture seems to want to hold you to when you make the statement: "I will stay together with you, in sickness . . . [no matter the situation] until death do us part." A much better intention or vow would be: *"It is my dominant intent to focus my thoughts in a positive direction so that I maintain my Connection with the Source and the Love that is really who I am. And in doing so, I will always present the best of myself to you. It is my desire that you ask the same for yourself. And it is my expectation that as each of us works to maintain our individual alignment with <u>who-we-really-are,</u> our relationship with one another will be one of continual and joyful expansion."*

### Do Nature's Laws Not Govern Our Mating?

**Jerry:** For much of my life I have been trying to determine what is the natural and right way for humans to approach relationships. I looked at the other beasts that roam the planet and have noticed that, for the most part, they are not much for monogamy. The elephant runs off all of the other male elephants, and the rooster will fight to the death any rooster that interferes with his flock of hens. I've wondered, *If humans were to behave more like the animals in regard to mating, would the human species become stronger and more powerful, like in "the survival of the fittest" with the animals?* From the perspective of the Non-Physical, is there a right and wrong approach to relationships? *So, my question is, what is natural?*

**Abraham:** There are enough natural forces at work to assure the sustaining of the human species: enough variation, enough diversity, enough balance. In the same way that your natural impulses to satisfy hunger and thirst assure your survival, your sexual impulses and mating impulses also assure your survival. *Our interest in the subject of human relationships is not because you need to adjust your behavior to ensure your survival, because the survival of your species is not in jeopardy. Our interest in human relationships is about your survival in joy.*

We have the benefit of being in full view of the Vibrational Escrows you have created from the contrasting experiences and relationships that you have lived, and it is our desire to help you find a way of achieving your own Vibrational alignment with those expanded creations so that you can live them, fully and joyously, now. *When something that you have lived has caused you to ask for an improved aspect, you must allow yourself the fullness of that desire or your joy is diminished. In simple terms, you have to keep up with what life has caused you to become or you cannot feel joy.*

These are the most correct, truthful, accurate, *natural* things that we know about you as you are expressing through your physical form:

- You are extensions of Source Energy.

- You are physically focused for the purpose of experiencing contrast.

- You are choosing to experience contrast for the purpose of new ideas and decisions about life.

- Those new ideas and decisions about life equal the expansion of the Universe.

- The expansion of the Universe is the inevitable consequence of life.

- When your physical life causes the Non-Physical part of you to expand, you must go with the expansion if you are to experience joy.

- Joy is the most natural tenet of that which you and we are.

- Relationships are the basis of your contrast.

- Therefore, relationships are the basis of all expansion.

- Therefore, relationships are the basis of your joy.

- If you do not find the thoughts that allow the joy, you are holding yourself back from *who-you-have-become.*

- Your relationships are your reason for your expansion.

- Your relationships are often your reason for disallowing your expansion.

- It is natural to be in a state of joy.

- It is natural to be in a state of growth.

- It is natural to be in a state of freedom.

- These are the most important things for you to understand about relationships.

### What Is Natural for Mating Humans?

**Jerry:** But which is more natural, having one mate or several? Should men have more than one wife at a time, or should women have more than one husband at a time? Even today, our cultures disagree about these things.

**Abraham:** Your question points directly at another very large, very flawed premise:

**Flawed Premise #13:** *There are right ways and wrong ways to live. And all people should discover and agree on what the right way of living is, and then that right way should be enforced.*

This flawed belief that there is only one right decision about any topic is at the heart of tremendous discord and upheaval. It is fortunate that you have no way of enforcing this flawed concept, for if you could, it would surely lead to the end of Beingness. In other words, since all expansion is born from the new intentions and ideas that are born from the contrast—elimination of the contrast would stop the expansion.

Do not worry, for that will never be the case, for the perfect balance of diversity has been very well established and flows with the *Laws of the Universe*. We are not discussing these things with you to preserve mankind or Eternity, because none of that is in jeopardy. We do discuss it with you, however, because your *joyful* survival is predicated upon your understanding of these things.

*When your life causes you to radiate a request into your Vibrational Escrow, your _Emotional Guidance System_ will help you find Vibrational alignment with it. And finding that alignment is necessary to your joyful fulfillment and expansion. And no laws that are apart from that have any bearing on you.*

The majority of the laws that surround you, both religious and secular, were written by those not in alignment with the Broader Perspective of Source. Your laws are usually written from the perspective of what is *not* wanted. And so, many people spend a tremendous amount of time in argument about which laws are right and which laws are wrong, and, in doing so, hold themselves apart from their expanded perspectives. And then they use the negative emotion that they feel (which exists because of their separation from Source) as their justification for their arguments.

When you no longer seek the final word on the rightness of your behaviors and instead seek alignment with the Source within you by finding thoughts, words, and deeds that fill you with love while you participate, you will understand that it is possible to live upon this planet with large numbers of other Beings—who believe and behave in a variety of ways—in peace.

*When you are able to focus in such a way as to allow your alignment with Source, even though others are choosing to behave differently than you are choosing, then you will truly be free from the bondage of attempting the impossible task of getting everyone to agree on one right way. _One right way would lead to endedness. Many right ways allow Eternal expansion._*

The reason why people believe that they need laws to control others around them is that they believe that the behavior of others can negatively impact them. But when you come to understand that nothing can come into your experience unless you invite it through thought, then you understand that you can release the impossible task of trying to control the behavior of others and replace it with the much simpler task of controlling the direction of your own thoughts.

We have come to remind you about the *Art of Allowing:* the *Art of Allowing* your Vibrational alignment with all that you have come to be and to desire. There is enough room in this very large, very diverse physical world for all that you are wanting. And every awful or abhorrent thing that you see exists only because someone is *disallowing* the Well-Being that would be there otherwise. The *Law of Attraction* is the *Law* that manages all things that are Vibrational. (And all things are Vibration.) You do not have to work at that *Law*—it just is. If you will put your attention toward understanding and applying the *Art of Allowing,* you will live in joy regardless of what others are doing. Just remember, during the time you are giving your attention to those who are not joyful, you are not practicing the *Art of Allowing.*

## Will Feeling Good Always Attract Good-Feelers?

**Questioner:** Is it a good idea for me to look for a mate who makes me feel good about myself?

**Abraham:** Of course. When others hold you as their object of attention and feel appreciation at the same time, it would feel very good to you, because they are in alignment with their own Source and are flooding that aligned Energy in your direction. That always feels good to both the flow-er of the appreciation and the recipient of the appreciation. But do not let your feeling good be dependent upon someone's positive attention shining on you. Show yourself that you can connect to the Non-Physical Stream whether you are being held in someone's positive flow or not. You have your own Connection, and when you practice it often, you will always be able to maintain your balance; whereas, if you wait for another to be in alignment and focused upon you, then your good feeling is dependent upon what someone else does, and that person may not always be in alignment, or you may not always be his or her only point of focus.

The reason why most relationships are much better feeling when they are new is because in the beginning, both partners are more inclined to look for the positive aspects in one another. Since your relationship is new, you are not yet aware of one another's flaws, but as time goes on, it is common to begin seeing more flaws and to be making less effort to be optimistic in your expectation.

When you are dependent upon no other for your Connection to Source, you will discover true freedom—freedom from the only thing that can ever bind you: resistance to *who-you-really-are*.

### Couldn't Anyone Become My Perfect Mate?

**Jerry:** If there were only two people on the earth, no matter who that other person was, couldn't we create out of that what we want? Couldn't we find within that one person, the perfect mate?

**Abraham:** First you must understand that if there were only two people on the earth, the experiences of contrast that you would have lived would be so limited that your desires would not be very evolved. However, under those limited conditions, your desire would also be limited, and so you would very likely be rather happy with that limited Being. But that is not the point you are getting at with your implausible hypothesis. Your point is, "If there is that which is wanted and that which is unwanted in every particle of the Universe, then can I not find *wanted* in *all* things? And if I focus upon wanted, won't the *Law of Attraction* bring me more wanted?" And the answer to that is *yes*.

Looking for positive aspects wherever you are always leads to an improved future. So even if you were enduring a mostly terrible relationship, out of that contrast would be born desires for improvement, which the Source within you would be holding as the object of its undivided attention. By deliberately focusing upon any small positive aspect you can find, you would then *allow* your alignment with the greater desires that had been born out of the contrast. And a consistent offering of that positive Vibration would deliver to you the physically manifested version. And, if (in your extreme hypothesis) there were only one other person on the planet, that desire would then have to be satisfied from that one person. Fortunately, you have a much larger, more cooperative playing field to draw from.

**Questioner:** When asked about what a perfect mate would be, someone whom I consider to be very wise said, "A perfect mate is someone who brings out the best in you, and also brings out the worst in you." What do you think about that?

**Abraham:** This person would be a bit like the contrasting world in general. In other words, whenever you know what you do not want, you always know more clearly what you do want. So he definitely would be helping you with the *Step One* part of the equation: *the asking.* Your success at making this a successful, and therefore happy, relationship would depend upon your ability to then focus upon the desire that this rascal helped you to launch. If your mate is evoking a steady stream of *I know what I don't want* awareness, and so you are launching steady rockets of desire about what you *do* want—and if you are then able to focus predominantly on what you *do* want—then, in your aligned state, your power of influence would be strong, and he would stop the negative prodding. But if his negative prodding was strong enough to stand in the face of your continuing *Allowing* state, then he could not remain in your experience. The *Law of Attraction* would put you in different places.

❦ ❦   ❦ ❦

# PART III

# Sexuality, and the *Law of Attraction:* Sexuality, Sensuality, and the Opinions of Others

## The Topics Are Sex, Sexuality, and Sensuality

**Jerry:** Sex, or sexuality, seems to be a sensitive topic in that it evokes guardedness and strong opinions from many who contemplate it. My first experience with anything remotely related to sexuality turned out very badly when a little girl and I were playing in a wooden box when we were about two years old. We got caught with our panties off, and we were both severely punished.

Also, as a child, I remember hearing my mother arguing with my father about sex. She told him that she had her three children, she was not interested in having sex with him, and he should find some other woman if it was important to him. Then later, I remember, as still very young children, the little boys and girls I knew and I were all having different sorts of sexual experiences with one another, but by the time I reached the age of actual sexual maturity, I guess because of the powerful stigma around the topic of sex, my concerns and fears and inhibitions were so strong that I would do just about anything to avoid the topic. It was a long time, for me, before my sexual barriers went down or were resolved and I was able to move into happy sexual experiences.

I would like to hear your perspective about the sexual aspects of physical human Beings to, perhaps, clarify the subject and leave people feeling better about it.

**Abraham:** As children, you are often met with adults who have lost Connection with their own sense of value, of Well-Being, and of worthiness; and from that lackful, disconnected state, they pass their guardedness on to you.

Over time, humans evaluate the subject of sexuality endlessly, passing new laws; amending old laws; struggling futilely to come to agreement with others about the correct attitude and approach to the subject and, even more futilely, to enforce the laws they create from their lackful positions. Your rules or laws about sexuality diverge from culture to culture, generation to generation, society to society, and religion to religion, but in nearly every case, your laws about this and every other subject tend to hinge on the economic impact of the time. And, most important, your sexual laws and rules, like all laws and rules, are made by those who are out of alignment with their Broader Perspective.

If humans were to understand that you are all Vibrational Beings and that the *Law of Attraction* is bringing to each of you only what you are a Vibrational Match to, you would not be so concerned about the behavior of others, for you would not fear their behavior negatively impacting you. But in your ignorance about how you *do* attract what comes, and in your fear that unwanted things *will* come, you make decisions and laws and rules that are not only impossible to enforce, but that foster even more of the behavior you seek to eliminate. *It is always true that the harder you push against what you do not want—the more of what you do not want comes into your experience.*

By far, the largest amount of pushing against the subject of sexuality comes from people of various religious groups who believe that *God* has spoken to humans and has given specific instructions regarding the topic. The inconsistency of the message man believes he has received accentuates the impossibility of receiving answers from the pure love of Source when the receiver is standing in a place of blame or guardedness. The very idea that "what I have received is correct, and what you or others have received is wrong" holds you in the place of resistance to the very Source from which you claim to have received it. Which leads us to the most important flawed premise of all:

**Flawed Premise #14:** *There is a God Who, having considered all things, has come to a final and correct conclusion about everything.*

This belief, or flawed premise, is at the root of man's continual assault on humanity. It is at the basis of your wars, your prejudices, your hatred, and your feelings of unworthiness; and it is your primary reason for disallowing your own Well-Being. This flawed premise is so important, and the ramifications of it are so immense, that we could write an entire book speaking only about man's distorted view of himself, of others, and of that which he calls *God.* This inaccurate conclusion—that Source (no matter what name you want to give it) is no longer expanding but instead stands at a place of completion, or perfection, demanding your physical compliance with its narrow rules—not only defies the *Laws of the Universe,* but then requires another flawed premise, and then another and another, to try to prop it up. From *outside* the Vibration of the love of his Source, man stands guarded and blameful and guilty and fearful, and then assigns those same lackful characteristics to that which he calls *God.*

Humanity continues to argue about the laws passed down from God as it bends and twists them to suit individual economic desires or needs. Often humans are informed by their religious leaders of the value, or necessity, of keeping these rules. You are told that the keeping of some rules will bring blessings, while the breaking of others will bring punishment; but when you notice that those who are breaking the laws seem to be thriving while those who strive to keep them most are often suffering greatly, you are told one of the greatest flawed premises of all:

***Flawed Premise #15:** You cannot know,
while you are still in your physical body, the true
reward or punishment for your physical actions. Your reward
or punishment will be shown to you after your physical death.*

The loving *Laws* that support *All-That-Exists* are *Laws* that are Universal and therefore always apply. And alignment with them is evident in every moment of alignment, just as misalignment with them is evident in every moment. What feels like love, *is*—and what feels like hate is not love.

There are many who want to live in the appropriate way, but sorting out proper behavior from the enormous lists of diversity leaves most people uncertain of the rightness of their path. Which leads to yet another flawed premise:

**Flawed Premise #16:** *By gathering data about the manifestations or results of the way the people of the earth have lived and are living, we can effectively sort them into absolute piles of right and wrong. And once those determinations have been made, we then have only to enforce those conclusions. And once we get everyone to agree with our determinations—and, more important, once we get them to comply with them—we will then have harmony on Earth.*

And so, more people die every day in the struggle to defend, or prove, which way of life is the correct way, with each group claiming to have the absolute approval and support of God. And, in not one bit of any of that is any true Connection to God.

You did not come into this physical body with the intention of taking all of the ideas that exist and whittling them down to a handful of agreed-upon ideas. In fact, that is the very opposite of your prebirth intention. Instead, you knew that you would be coming into an environment of extreme variety, and that from that platform of difference and choices would be born more new-and-improved ideas. You understood that the Eternal nature of that which humans call *God* would be enhanced by your participation. You knew that this platform of enormous contrast would be the foundation of the Eternal expansion that exists within that which humans call Eternity. *There is no ending to the expansion of God, and physical humans' participation cannot be separated from that expansion.*

The most destructive part of humans' confusion about their Connection with God or Source is that in their need to find and defend their values, they must push against the values of others. And the very nature of focusing upon and pushing against unwanted aspects of others prevents their alignment with the very *goodness* and *Source* that they seek. And then they blame the differences in others for the emptiness they feel. Which leads us to another flawed premise:

**Flawed Premise #17:** *Only very special people, like the founder of <u>our</u> group, can receive the right message from God. And all other messages from all other messengers are therefore incorrect.*

It is interesting that in the midst of a conversation about sexuality, we would not only uncover one of the biggest flawed premises of all, but that the subject of sexuality is also the avenue through which the existence of humans hinges. A basic feeling of unworthiness, due to the lack of Connection with *Source,* is at the root of the confusion around the subject of sexuality.

It is a rare human who has found what he believes to be the appropriate way to behave, who has then also mustered the self-discipline to behave that way, because the natural instincts that are inspired from a much Broader knowing run counter to the restricted behavior assigned by human Beings.

## Are Our Sexual Laws Decreed
## by Non-Physical Dimensions?

**Jerry:** So what is *natural* for me? I remember, as years went by, that I always wanted to understand not only what is *natural,* but what might go against the higher laws. For instance, as I observed or read about cultures around the world, it seemed like every one, no matter how primitive or how supposedly advanced, had taboos and rules—which controlled the newer people coming in—regarding sex. And so, I wondered if we bring any of that from our higher knowing or from our *Inner Beings.*

**Abraham:** No taboos or rules are coming from your *Inner Being* or from your higher knowing or from Non-Physical, but instead, they are the product of your physical vulnerability. Without exception, every law—religious or secular—comes from a perspective of lack, from a position of trying to protect or guard someone from something. If you were really paying attention to what is happening regarding these laws, you would realize that the laws do not deter the lawbreakers. They only hinder those who would not break the laws anyway, restrict freedom, and add confusion to the lives of those who seek approval from others through conformity.

Can you hear the birds? [Abraham is commenting on sounds of nature that are audible from inside the house.] That is a very *sexual* call. A moment ago, the rooster was crowing so loudly that you considered not continuing with the recording. In other words, your world is filled with Beings who are all receiving direction from Non-Physical. And yet, it is only the humans who are guarded and resistant regarding the subject of sexuality; it is only the humans who are coming from this extreme place of lack regarding the subject of sexuality. And, from your perspective of lack, from your concern that you may be doing something wrong, from your concern that has been fostered within you from those who have gone before, you are, most of you, in a place of great confusion and not very much joy.

### Sexuality Is Guided by Impulses, Not Laws

**Jerry:** Okay. So there are no rules from the Non-Physical dimension telling us how to behave sexually here in physical form, and so when we are born into our physical bodies, we didn't come knowing any rules because we weren't sent with them. Is that why children are so unguarded and behave in ways that adults see as too loose or too careless? And is that why adults then feel a need to rein them in or control them?

**Abraham:** You were not born into your physical body holding the memory of lists of right and wrong because those lists do not exist, but you were born with an effective *Guidance System. The emotions that you feel, without exception, are indicators of the Vibrational alignment—or variance—between the thought your human* *brain is focused upon and the perspective of your Broader Non-Physical Perspective regarding the same subject.*

Since the Source within you is Eternally expanding, your understanding, perspective, intentions, and the knowledge of that part of you is Eternally expanding as well. That is the reason there cannot be a static list of right and wrong or good and evil for you to measure your experience against. Instead, you have personal, individual, loving, accurate feedback, thought by thought, moment by moment, to help you know when you are in alignment with that Broader Perspective or when you are not. *There is not only one guidance list handed down from Source for all, but individual Guidance for all physical Beings, in all points in time and space, and regarding all situations.*

If, in your desire to socialize the new arrivals into your society, you are unaware of your own *Guidance System,* and therefore unaware of theirs, then you embark upon the impossible task of determining which actions are the right actions. You also have the even more impossible task of enforcing those decisions.

The reason why so many people feel a need to control the behavior of others is because they believe that others have the power to assert themselves into their experience. When you remember that nothing can come into your experience without your Vibrational invitation of it, then you do the simple work of paying attention to your own Vibrational offering, and you save yourself the enormous and impossible task of controlling the behavior of others. *When you remember that the varied behavior of others adds to the balance and the Well-Being of your planet even if they offer behavior that you do not approve of; and that you do not have to participate in the unwanted behavior, and will not—unless you give your attention to it—you become more willing to allow others to live as they choose.*

The need to control others always stems from a basic misunderstanding of the *Laws of the Universe* and of the role that you have intended to play with others with whom you share your planet. But there is another very big flawed premise that arises here:

**Flawed Premise #18:** *By ferreting out the undesirable elements in our society, we can eliminate them. And in their absence, we will be freer.*

True freedom is the absence of resistance; true freedom is the presence of alignment—true freedom is the way you feel when you are no longer disallowing your complete alignment, or blending, with the Broader Non-Physical part of you. Therefore, it is not possible to be in the act of pushing against something unwanted and be blended with *who-you-really-are* and what you want at the same time. *You cannot be in the state of pushing against what you <u>do not</u> want and be in harmony with what you <u>do</u> want at the same time. And so, you will never get to a better-feeling state by trying to control others, no matter how well-meaning you believe your motives to be.*

You did not come knowing rules of correct behavior, but you certainly came feeling impulses. In other words, just as you have the impulse to drink when you are thirsty in order to keep your body replenished or to eat when you are hungry to keep your body fueled, so the sensation, or the urging, of sexuality comes forth naturally for the perpetuation of the species upon your planet.

### What If Humans Behaved, Sexually, Like the Wild Animals?

**Jerry:** So, getting back to the animals, who do seem to behave from their Non-Physical Guidance or *instinct,* as we have come to call it . . . our rooster and his hens have no written laws, or rules, that they are conforming to; it's just what comes from within them. And so, if we could be born into this planet and start fresh like that, without rules, it seems like we, too, should be able to operate from our *Inner Being* without the need of outside restrictions. But, instead, we are born into societies and cultures that already have rules and controls that they insist we conform to.

**Abraham:** What we most want you to understand is that, as humans, you, too, do have Guidance that is coming forth from within. And your Guidance, your innate knowing, your sense of self—indeed, the Eternal nature of *who-you-are*—is what is dominant within you. And while you do believe that you are hindered by the controls set forth by other humans, we want you to know that this control is not as large or as hindering as you believe, because your innate Non-Physical impulses are even stronger.

Even though your societies have imposed endless rules or laws regarding your sexual behavior, many more of you break those rules—and always have broken those rules—than keep them. That is because your Non-Physical impulses are so strong. If your government, or some controlling agency, were to tell you that you were no longer allowed to eat food—your natural impulses of survival would prevail, and you would find a way to eat.

You and your world do not need this book in order to free your behavior from the binding laws and rules and misunderstandings about sexuality, because your natural impulses are so strong that you really are not behaving as if you feel bound by them. In other words, your natural instincts and impulses are so strong that they do lead your behavior. But then you suffer emotional discord as you then measure your behavior against those unrealistic rules that have been created from your place of attempting to control behaviors. In other words, you behave naturally, but then you feel bad about it.

*Your societies will never find the happiness they seek—or know the deliciousness of true freedom—as long as they believe in controlling the behavior of one another. It is the control of your thought, and the alignment with your Broader Perspective, that you are really seeking.*

## What about When Society Disapproves of Sexual Individuality?

**Jerry:** So what if you feel good when you think about a specific action, but when you consider what others think about your action, you don't feel good? Then what would you suggest?

**Abraham:** We would say that now you are off track because you are attempting to guide your actions by the opinions of others outside of you, when the only guidance that counts is the Guidance that you feel as your thought, in the moment, harmonizes—or does not harmonize—with the Broader Perspective of your Source.

No other human really knows the intentions you held as you came forth from Non-Physical. They have not walked in your shoes through the thousands of interactions you have experienced, and they were not a part of the rockets of desire that you have launched as you have lived your life. They are not privy to the Vibrational Reality that you have created through the living of life, and they cannot feel the harmony or discord—the allowing or resisting— that you feel through your own emotions.

Your question is an important one because through it you are trying to understand which of your emotions to trust or follow: the good-feeling emotion that came in response to your personal thoughts about your personal experience, or the bad-feeling emotion that came in response to your awareness of the disapproval of another.

Nothing could be more important than coming to recognize the existence of your *Emotional Guidance System* and how it works, for without it you have no consistent guidance. The emotions you feel, in any moment, are pointing out to you the agreement or disagreement between you and your Source regarding the thought that is active in you at the moment of the emotion. If you can understand that through life, before you entered this body and since, your *Inner Being* has become the Vibrational summation of all that you have lived and now stands as the Vibrational equivalent to all that is good—and if you can then understand that your emotions are giving you feedback about how your current thought blends with that all-knowing, Pure, Positive Energy viewpoint of Source— then and only then can you fully appreciate your emotions.

So when you feel negative emotion, it always means that your currently active thought is out of alignment with the knowledge of Source. In other words, when you find fault with yourself, when you decide that you are inappropriate or unworthy, you will always feel negative emotion—because the Source within you only feels love toward you. When you disapprove of others, you will always feel negative emotion—because the Source within you only loves others. If you will remember that whenever you feel negative emotion, it always means you are in disagreement with Source, then you can deliberately reframe your thoughts until you come into alignment. That is the way to effectively utilize your *Guidance System.*

When people replace this very personal Guidance by attempting to modify their behavior to please other people, they very soon discover the inconsistency of that guidance and soon find themselves confused about what to do. Many people have lost conscious Connection with their own *Guidance Systems,* and so instead of deliberately focusing their thoughts into harmony and alignment with their Source and their power—instead of making sure that they are steadily tuned to the Vibration of their clarity and love and power— they turn their attention to the results of what they and the people around them have been thinking. In other words, they examine and catalog and pigeonhole and evaluate and judge the results of the Vibrational creating that is happening around them, putting those results into categories of *good* and *bad, right* and *wrong.* And in all of that data, they lose their way.

There are so many differing opinions and so many extenuating circumstances and so many motives that make it impossible to sort out the rightness or wrongness of interpersonal behavior in your societies. And even when you come to, more or less, general consensus of what you agree upon as a society as the appropriate ways to live, you have no way of convincing all others of the rightness of your opinion. And even when you come together and pronounce laws against "inappropriate" behavior, you have no way of enforcing those laws. . . . *While your societies continue to try to dictate and enforce human behavior to please the majority—because of your diversity, it continues to be an uncomfortable struggle that, again and again, falls of its economic weight. There simply is not enough money in the world to buck the natural currents of individual freedom and independence of thought.*

When people have forgotten that this is an inclusion-based Universe, and that the *Law of Attraction* is the manager who is arranging every detail of every rendezvous that occurs, they fear something that can never be: *they fear that unwanted things can assert themselves into their experience.* But when you remember that nothing uninvited ever comes into your experience, and that every invitation of both wanted and unwanted comes because you have given considerable thought to the essence of it, then you can begin to utilize your own powerful *Emotional Guidance System* with the assurance that you *do* create your own reality.

If people would simply pay attention to the harmony or disharmony within themselves—which is offered to them in the form of positive or negative emotion—they would be able to eliminate the arduous and impossible task of trying to control the behavior of others.

*By deliberately focusing your thoughts in the direction of your Broader understanding, and no longer wasting time and money on things you cannot control, you will not only come into alignment with Source and feel the relief of that in your emotions—but all things wanted can then come to you.*

So getting back to your powerful question . . . your thought about a behavior or action that brought you pleasure—regardless of the opinions of others who stand upon their endless opinions and rules and disapproving platforms—is a thought that the Source within you agrees with. And your thought of your own inappropriateness that made you feel bad, because of your assumed disapproval of others (whether real or imagined) is a thought that the Source within you does not agree with.

To sort out all of the behaviors of your societies, past and present; to sort out all of the opinions of people around your world; to review all of the laws; to understand how the laws came about; to evaluate the evolution of the laws; to try to live up to all of them, or enforce them . . . is confusing and overwhelming and impossible.

*To know if <u>Source, Infinite Intelligence, Inner Being, God</u> agrees or disagrees with the thought, word, or action you are involved in—you have only to notice if it feels good or bad.*

To find your peace regarding anything, it is necessary for you to set aside your desire to find approval from others and to seek approval from self. And you do that by starting from the inside out—by acknowledging that you want to feel good, and that you want to have a life experience that is in harmony with what is good. And if you start there, it is our absolute promise to you that you will never find yourself in a situation where the action that you are experiencing, or even contemplating, will put you in a position of feeling that you have betrayed your greater sense of right and wrong.

### Who Gets to Set Humans' Sexual Hierarchy?

**Jerry:** It seems to me, as I have evaluated sexuality within our culture, that we have what might be called the high priest, who *doesn't* engage in sex; then there are the common folks, who *do* engage in sex (but only for the purpose of creating children); and then, on the lower end of the hierarchy, there would be those who would engage in sex for pleasure. But it seems to me that we all have some of all of that—

**Abraham:** We have to interrupt you here because all of those ideas come from a perspective of lack, from humans believing in their unworthiness.

Your physical life experience is a life of sensuality. You come forth into this physical realm with the sensual eyes with which to see, the sensual ears with which to hear, the sensual nose with which to smell, the sensual skin with which to feel, and the sensual tongue with which to taste. This Leading Edge time-space reality is about the intricate Vibrational interpretations that your physical senses provide, and all of that is for the enhancement of your physical experience.

If you will pay attention to your emotions, they will help you find the appropriateness of your behavior, and you will come to understand the worthiness that is at the core of you. It is not necessary, or even possible, to pinpoint the turning point when humans stopped believing in their value and worthiness. It has been a gradual erosion caused by the disallowance of Connection with Source because of the comparison of human experience in search of the one "right" answer or the one "right" behavior. And now, a feeling of unworthiness runs rampant on your planet, and much of human thought is directed toward lack, which only promotes more disallowance of alignment with Source and with love and with Well-Being.

You are here in your physical bodies as extensions of Source Energy, experiencing specific contrast and coming to specific new decisions about the goodness of life, and every time your experience poses a question to you—an equivalent answer is born in the experience of Source. Every time your experience poses a problem to you—an equivalent solution is born in the experience of Source. And so, because of your willingness to live and explore and experience contrast, you are giving birth to constant new rockets of desire—and *All-That-Is* expands because of what you are living.

*When it becomes your dominant intention to find good-feeling thoughts, then you become one who is most often a Vibrational Match to the Source within you, and the good feeling that will then be usually present within you is your indication that you are fulfilling your reason for being and that you are continuing to keep up with the expansion of your own Being.*

Every experience causes you to expand, and your positive emotion is your indication that you are keeping up with that new expansion. Negative emotion is your indication that the greater part of you has moved to an expanded place—but you are holding back. And so, by paying attention to the way you feel, and by continually reaching for the best-feeling thoughts you can find, you will establish a rhythm of alignment that will help you immediately realize when you are straying from the goodness that you have become.

It is our absolute promise to you that you will never be able to take action that is contrary to the joyful, loving, God-Source Being within you without feeling very strong negative emotion. . . . There are many people who are completely out of alignment with the Source within them, who stand in condemnation of others while asserting their claim on righteousness. But the anger that burns within them is evidence of their disallowance of the very rightness they are making claim to. *Anger and hatred and condemnation are not symbols of alignment with God—but indicators of misalignment with that which you call God.*

Some would say, "Then the feeling of guilt that I have must mean that I am doing something evil or wrong." But we want you to understand that your negative emotion simply means that the thought that is vibrating within you does not match the Vibration of your Source. Source continues to love you. When *you* do not love you, you feel the discord.

If we were standing in your physical shoes and we were contemplating an action that caused negative emotion, we would not proceed with the action until we had resolved the negative emotion. We would make sure that we had come into alignment with Source before proceeding. *By feeling for the improved thought, in time, and usually in a short time, you will feel the harmony of your Source; and you will know the appropriateness of your behavior. We would not look for the long lists of right and wrong, but instead, we would feel for the emotion of alignment with Source.*

Negative emotion does not mean that you are not good. It means that your currently active thought does not harmonize with the currently active thoughts of Source on the same subject. If you have come to believe that sexual interaction is wrong and you are about to engage in sexual interaction, your negative emotion is not confirming that sexual interaction is wrong. It is confirming that your opinion of your behavior and of yourself in this moment does not harmonize with how Source feels about you. Stop and reach for loving, approving thoughts about yourself and feel the discord disappear.

Usually, by the time you have spent 50 or 60 or 70 years in your body, you come to the very clear awareness that you cannot please them all. In fact, you usually understand that you cannot please very many of them, because each of them wants something different from you. Attempting to guide yourself through the approval of others is futile and painful. But you may trust your inner Guidance. In fact, it is really the only thing that you *can* trust, because it holds the complete understanding of *who-you-really-are, who-you-have-become,* and where you stand in Vibrational relationship with that expanded Being.

When you understand your relationship with the Source within you and you are aware of your own *Emotional Guidance System*— which continually indicates your Vibrational relationship with Source—it will not be possible for you to stray from the wholeness and goodness and the worthiness that is you.

### How Can We Coordinate Our Sexual Co-creations?

**Jerry:** It seems to me that humans have, within them, an innate urge to procreate, as well as an innate desire to enjoy sensuality. And I believe we also have an innate desire to create through thought, but the subject of sexuality really points to the idea of co-creation, where the desires and beliefs and intentions of two people are now involved. How can two different people who are moving through time and experiences continue to co-create in harmony? How can I coordinate my desires with the desires of my mate, since both of us are changing?

**Abraham:** As we discussed in the last question, it is important that your desire for harmony with your mate not become a desire to seek approval from that person. There is no more destructive force to relationships than the feeling of the loss of freedom in the effort to find agreement. Which leads us to another flawed premise:

*Flawed Premise #19: A good relationship is*
*one in which the dominant intention of each person*
*involved is to find agreement and harmony with the other.*

How could two people looking to find harmony with each other possibly be the wrong basis for a good relationship and a happy life? Both people have created their own Vibrational Escrow (Vibrational Reality) to which they must seek harmony if they are to be happy. When finding harmony with your mate takes precedence over finding harmony with your Inner Self, there is a strong probability that discord between you and Source will occur. That feeling of discord is then translated as a feeling of loss of freedom; and then your partner, with whom you truly want to find harmony, begins to feel less good. Your loss of connection to your own Source feels off to you, and *is* off, and so then (without wanting to) you begin to resent the partner whom you are trying to please. In short, there is no substitution for alignment with Source.

Again, you are looking for love in all the wrong places. We are not suggesting that you should not want to get along well with your mate. But we are strongly suggesting the powerful benefit of seeking, first, alignment with Source. *When you find alignment with the Source within you, you also find alignment with your furthermost expansion. And when you are in alignment with <u>who-you-really-are</u> and all that you have become, you are then automatically in harmony with the best of your relationship with your partner.*

Couples, or anyone involved in co-creating of any kind, who attempt harmony by trying first to please each other always discover the flaw in that premise. *If you are not selfish enough to seek and find harmony with your Source, you have nothing to give your partner anyway.*

If you see it as your job to keep your partner happy, and so you work hard and behave in ways that please your mate, you are actually setting your mate up for ultimate unhappiness because you are training that person to look to you and your behavior in order to feel good rather than seeking personal alignment with Source. And no matter how good you are at pleasing, and no matter how hard you try, you do not make a good substitute for your partner's alignment with Source.

The message that you want to convey to the others with whom you are co-creating is this: "I will never hold you responsible for the way I feel. I have the power to focus myself into alignment with my Source, and therefore I have the power to keep myself feeling good." If that is your true intention, then you have discovered the path, the *only* path, to true freedom and true happiness. But if your happiness is dependent upon the intentions or beliefs or behaviors of any other, you are trapped, for you cannot control any of that.

### Fear of Sex Spoils the Pleasure of Being Touched

**Jerry:** Abraham, I would like to read to you some questions that people have asked you. These are real-life examples that are happening with people, and I'd like to hear your responses relative to the *Laws* and processes that you've been teaching us.

A young woman says: "My mother and I are both uncomfortable with sex. We don't like hearing about it, reading about it, seeing it on television, or participating in it. I guess, as a result of my mother's strong negative feelings about sex, I now have fear anytime my mate even touches me that it might turn to having sex. I want a good marriage, but how can I enjoy the sensual part, or the touching part, without this fear that it will push on into the sexual part?"

**Abraham:** Most anyone reading or hearing the perspective of this woman would have a strong reaction to her words. Some would feel sorry for her husband to have a wife who is so repulsed by the idea of sexual interaction, while others would identify with her feeling about it. If this woman is married to someone who feels differently about the sexual experience than she does, then one of them will always be uncomfortable regarding the subject.

The most important thing that we want you to understand (and it is usually the most difficult thing for most people to understand) is that this conversation, and ultimately this solution, is not about the *action* of sexuality, for there is no rule about right and wrong sexual behavior. A strong pattern of negative emotion attached to a specific subject means that the thoughts you have chronically activated about that subject strongly disagree with the perspective of your Source.

For example, if, as a young girl (age is irrelevant, but these things usually begin when you are very young), you felt strong disapproval projected toward you in response to your words or behavior regarding the subject, you most likely have concluded that you were inappropriate to be offering those words or that behavior, or even those thoughts. You called the empty feeling *guilt,* and you accepted it as evidence of your wrongdoing or wrong speaking or wrong thinking. But the guidance that your *Emotional Guidance System* was offering was very different from that: Your feeling of guilt was, instead, a simple indicator that your conclusion about your inappropriateness was a very different opinion from the Source within you. In other words, you were condemning you—and your Source was not.

There is nothing that you innately want more than to recognize your own value and goodness, and when you harbor chronic thoughts that disallow that, you feel bad. If you have decided that a particular behavior is wrong—you will always feel worse if you perform it. If you have decided that a particular behavior is good—you will always feel better if you perform it. But your life becomes very complicated as you try to sort that out through putting behaviors in categories of *right* and *wrong,* of *good* or *bad.*

For example, if you believe that a good wife is one who tries to cooperate with her husband, you would feel bad by not yielding to his sexual desires. If you believe that sexual interaction is wrong, then yielding to your husband's sexual desires would also feel bad, so whether you say *yes* or *no* to his request, you feel bad. It is an impossible thing for you to sort out. And so, in time, you decide that his sexual desires are inappropriate.

But we want you to understand that none of these emotions that you have been feeling have anything to do with the rightness or the wrongness of his request or behavior. Your emotions are always, and only, about whether your thoughts about a subject align with the thoughts of your *Inner Being.* And when you decide you are inappropriate, you are always out of alignment with your Source. When you decide that your husband is inappropriate, you are always out of alignment with your Source. If you decide that your mother was wrong to influence you on the subject of sexuality, you are out of alignment with Source.

Let us say that, through the life experience that you have lived, you have decided that you do not want to participate in a particular activity, sexual or otherwise. And let us also say that you spend no time thinking about what you do not want regarding the subject, so there is no active Vibration within you about it. Under those conditions, the powerful *Law of Attraction* would bring to you a partner who is in complete agreement with you, and you would have no struggle in living your compatible life.

Now, let us say that, through the life that you have lived, you have decided that you do not want to participate in a particular activity. You made that decision when you were young. In fact, you learned it from your mother, whom you trusted. This feels like an important decision to you. You read books about it. You seek counsel about it. You are very, very clear about what you do not want; and you justify that decision often. In this situation it would not be possible for the *Law of Attraction* to bring you a partner who agrees with you because the Vibration that you predominantly offer on this topic does not agree with your own decision. So you would attract partners who ask or demand of you the exact opposite of what you have decided that you want.

It is not our desire to guide you toward or away from sexual activity, but we do want you to understand that this is another case where "you cannot get there from there." You cannot continue to offer a Vibration that consists mostly of what you *do not* want and get what you *do* want. And we also would like you to understand that when you pay attention to the way you feel, and deliberately choose more thoughts that feel good while you think them, you will begin to recognize the nature of your Broader Non-Physical desires. *The majority of negative emotions that you feel are not because the subject of your thought is wrong, but instead, because you are condemning something that your Source does not condemn. Your Source is one of love, not one of condemnation.*

And so, over time, as you come more into alignment with the Vibration of the Source within you, it is our promise to you that your feelings of sensuality will return. For you have come forth into this physical body wanting to explore and enjoy the delicious nature of your physical beingness. We have never seen a physical human who was in *alignment* with Source who was repulsed by physical interaction. Repulsion is an indication of *disconnection.*

### We Can Always Have a Fresh Start

**Jerry:** Abraham, before meeting you, I described life as like moving along a path that had many possible branches that forked this way and that way. I could choose this branch of the path or that one; and if I ever found myself at a point where life didn't feel right, I could just backtrack to the last fork in the road and then, perhaps, choose a better path. But it seems like you are saying that I don't have to double back, and that I could just start fresh at any time.

**Abraham:** The thing that your analogy does not factor in is that during the time on your trail that you were not having a good time, as it was not feeling right, you were sending out Vibrational rockets of desire for the equivalent improvement or solutions—and in doing so, you added to your Vibrational Escrow your newly amended desires. Further, the Non-Physical part of you became that expanded Being living that better experience. It is neither necessary nor possible for you to backtrack to a former physical perspective. Life has caused you to move on. And, most important, that expanded version of you is calling you; and if you will listen, a well-lighted and easy-to-navigate path will appear before you.

## How Does One Regain the Frequency of Pleasurable Sexuality?

**Jerry:** On the other side of the question posed by the young woman we just discussed, there is a gentleman who says: "For the first three months of our marriage, my wife and I had sex three or four times every day. But now, after a few years, it has actually reached the point that the activity of sex is distasteful to my wife. And so, if I don't make it happen, it just doesn't happen. She is not interested in any form of mental stimulation, like words, films, or books. She won't allow anything that would shift her focus in that direction. I don't want to have sex with her if she doesn't enjoy it, because if it's not pleasurable for her, it's not pleasurable for me. *What thoughts must I change in order to change the experience that I am having?*"

**Abraham:** Many people find themselves in troubling situations where there seem to be no viable solutions: "Since my wife doesn't want sexual interaction, then my choices are: (1) I could go along with not having sex . . . which doesn't feel good to me; (2) I could leave my wife and find another partner who is more compatible on the subject, like we were in the beginning . . . but I don't want to leave her; (3) I could stay in the marriage but find another sexual partner . . . but I don't want to betray or deceive my mate, and I am certain she would not condone my doing that; (4) I could try to convince her or even assert pressure to move her in the direction of my desires . . . but that is uncomfortable and suppresses my own sexual desire."

The reason none of the choices just mentioned afford any viable solution is because none of them are addressing the real problem. When two people are in love (like so many people describe at the beginning of their relationships), their positive attention to each other, and their positive expectation about their relationship, is often a catalyst that causes them both to align with their respective *Inner Beings*. So you could say that they are each using each other as their excuse to be in alignment with *who-they-really-are*. And that alignment translates as harmony. *There is no greater symbol of co-creative harmony than the physical blending of two people in sexual interaction.*

Of course, it is possible to interact physically without one or both of the parties involved being in alignment with Source, but when that physical/Source alignment is in place, then the physical intertwining is divine.

Of course, you would want your mate to be in alignment with her Source for many more reasons than because she would be more likely to be willing to engage in sexual interaction with you, but, in any case, her connection to Source is what we would focus upon.

You do not have the power to align others with their *Inner Being*. You only have the power to align yourself with your own. You cannot focus upon your sexual incompatibility and be in alignment with your *Inner Being* at the same time. You cannot notice that your mate is not in alignment with her *Inner Being* and be in alignment with your *Inner Being* the same time. You cannot focus upon the absence of something that you desire and be in alignment with your *Inner Being* at the same time. Your solution hinges upon your ability to find thoughts about sexuality with your mate while at the same time being in alignment with your Source.

In short, as you often find thoughts about sexual interaction with your mate that feel good to you while you think them, you will be in alignment with the Source within you and with your desires. When you think about sexual interaction with your mate and you feel guilty or blameful or disappointed, you are not in alignment with your Source or with your desires. When you think about sexual interaction with your mate and you feel eager or happy or sensual, you are in alignment with your Source and with your desire. So, over time, as you are able to focus upon the subject and remain in alignment with your Source, the powerful *Law of Attraction* will find more and more compatible rendezvous points, and you will rediscover your early passion with your mate.

It is possible that your mate could remain resistant to her own alignment, and if that is the case, then the *Law of Attraction* will bring to you another mate who matches the Vibration that you have developed. However, once you are consistently holding your mate as your positive object of attention while you are in complete alignment with your *Inner Being,* it is much more likely that she will return to her natural alignment.

Engaging in sexual interaction, as inspired from Connection with your *Inner Being,* is a delicious physical experience, while engaging in sexual interaction out of a feeling of commitment or responsibility is not.

In short, if you do not allow yourself to get into a feeling of shortage or lack because of something that another does, and you are able to maintain your alignment with the Source within you, what you desire must come to you. And, in this situation, where it is clear that this man cares about the feelings of his mate, his alignment will most likely inspire hers.

So this conversation is not about how to get yourself into a position where you can get from another something that you desire. Instead, it is about how to align yourself with Source regardless of what another is doing. And then, by your own consistent alignment with Source, you *may* inspire the alignment of your mate. And the by-product of all of that alignment is—as the man discovered in the early days of his relationship—a desire to become one with the positive object of your attention.


### Sex, Religion, and Mental-Hospital Incarcerations?

**Jerry:** Some years ago I was visiting a group of friends who were psychiatrists and psychologists who told me, in essence, that the majority of people who were incarcerated in a mental hospital where they worked, near Spokane, Washington, were there as a result of their confusion either about religion or sex. And I'm sure it was not only their confusion that put them there, but also their behavior.

**Abraham:** That is not surprising, because both the subject of religion and the subject of sexuality point toward the origin of human Beings. Many people look to religion to help them understand why they are here. They want to understand their purpose for being here, and they want to fulfill that purpose. And the subject of sexuality is the means through which they came forth into their physical bodies.

Most religions offer tremendous patterns of "pushing against" as they scrutinize human behavior looking for evidence of wrong-doing and sin. And often that perceived wrongdoing is pointed toward sexual behavior. Every thought that devalues self, even if it is spoken from a religious platform, causes separation between the human physical self and the Non-Physical *Inner Being*. And that is, in fact, what *confusion* is. Only people severely separated from Source would offer an act of hostility, violence, or sexual aggression. There is a powerful connection there: *since they are focused upon lack, they take the subjects that are of greatest importance to them and focus upon the lack side of it.*

## Why Do People Use *God* and *Sex* in Vain?

**Jerry:** And another thing I have noticed is that, for some reason, in our society when people are really angry or violent or threatening, or are really trying to hurt someone's feelings, they use words that are related to sex or religion as curse words. It seems like the worse they feel, the more they use sexual or religious words in a derogatory way to get their point across.

**Abraham:** That is because when they are focused upon lack—and therefore disconnected from Source—they choose the subjects that are the most meaningful or important and find the lack side of them.

## Why Does the Media Broadcast Pain,
## but Censor Pleasure?

**Jerry:** I also notice that in our culture it seems perfectly appropriate for television and movies to depict the maiming of people, and destruction and gore—anything horrible as far as destroying the human body—while it seems inappropriate to show human sexuality and pleasure. I've never understood why our culture has come to the place where it can stand hate and anger and pain, but doesn't want to see pleasure.

**Abraham:** It is not a matter of their wanting to see hate, anger, and pain, and not wanting to see pleasure. In fact, the opposite of that is true: people really *do* want to feel good, and they want to see things that are successful and beautiful and pleasurable.

Many people are attracting to themselves unwanted things by virtue of their attention to those unwanted things. A misunderstanding of the *Laws of the Universe* is at the heart of this conversation as the people of your society wage wars against the things they do not want: war against terror, war against AIDS, war against teenage pregnancy, war against violence, war against cancer—and every one of those things is getting bigger because attention to unwanted creates more unwanted.

Your moviemakers, whether they understand the *Law of Attraction* or not, understand that people do gravitate more toward viewing unwanted things than wanted. And we submit that the reason that is true is because there are strong active Vibrations in most people about what they do not want. If you were to engage the average person in conversation about what is going on with his life, you would find him much more articulate in expressing the things that are not working well—things that are unjust and things that need to be changed—than he would be able to express the beauty of his life and world.

Also, once you have decided that the world is leaning toward anger and hate, you are no longer a Vibrational Match to the beauty of the world—and the world, as you attract, then leans in the direction of your belief. Anyone who begins to make lists of the positive aspects of the world around them will train their Vibration and therefore their own point of attraction to more of that. Meanwhile, the people who make movies will continue to make the movies that people are attracting from them.

We would like to help you remember that if you are waiting around for your society to get straightened out before you have a happy life experience, you will have a very long wait. If you are waiting for anybody else in your experience to get straightened out before you have a happy experience, you will have a very long wait.

You are not here to *discover* that which is perfect. You are here to *create* or to *attract* that which is perfect. As the contrast of your life, and even of what you are calling unpleasant movies, helps you know what you *do not* want, you also understand more clearly what you *do* want. *Focus upon what you do want, become a Vibrational Match to what you do want, train your point of attraction to what you do want—and watch your personal world become that.*

### Monogamy: Is It Natural or Unnatural?

**Questioner:** Where I'm stuck is on the whole issue of *monogamy.* That is the way I was raised, and so I assume that that's a value of mine, but I've noticed a lot of pain and fear associated with it. First of all, you have to find someone who wants the same thing, and then you have to control the person's wanting, which is not fun by itself, and . . .

**Abraham:** Not only is it not fun to attempt control over another, it is not possible. People often believe that what they really want is just some final ruling on the rightness or wrongness of monogamy so that they could then keep the rule or break the rule, but at least they would know what the rule is. And so, in your societies that rule has moved back and forth many times. It varies today depending upon what part of the world you are living in. But we want you to understand that it was never your intention as you came into the physical from Non-Physical to find one way of living and convince or coerce all others to abide. You understood that the world is big enough to accommodate vast differences in desires, beliefs, and the creation of lifestyles.

Which brings us to the first point of this question: *I need to find someone who wants what I want.* Coming together with another who is in agreement with the desires that you hold does make for good relationships. And, surely it is obvious that there are enough people with whom you share your planet that it should not be too difficult to find someone who is a match to you and what you want. But the thing that hinders most people—as they are looking to find that other person who matches the things that they desire—is that they cannot find that person unless they themselves are a match to their own desires.

People who worry about finding someone who will remain true to them cannot find such a person because the most active thoughts within them are worrisome thoughts of betrayal. People are finding it difficult to find the mate of their dreams not because that person is not out there, but because of their own contradiction to their own desire in the thoughts they offer about the subject every day.

*When you consistently offer thoughts about your future relationship that feel good while you think them, that means you are consistently matching the desires that you have discovered as you have lived life. And under those conditions, only someone in agreement with your desires could come to you. Under those conditions, no need for control is necessary.*

**Questioner:** So is it our "natural" nature to have only one relationship over a lifetime? Or is that something that was imposed on us by culture or religion?

**Abraham:** It was your intent to interact with many others on many subjects. And whether you choose the subject of sexuality to be something that you experience with only one, or whether it is something that you want to experience with more than one, or with many, it is an individual thing. And your ideas about it are continually changing.

It is worth noting, however, that the rules and laws that are meant to restrict behavior are always born out of the disconnection from Source. In other words, as your officials or leaders or rulers legislate laws or rules in an effort to eliminate something from society, their attention is usually upon the aspect of society that they do *not* want. And so, even though they make laws and attempt to enforce them, they have but minuscule control, because they are fighting the natural laws of nature. *The most powerful force inherent in all who exist is the acknowledgment of personal freedom.*

It is not possible for you to form your ideas about what a wonderful relationship really is if you have no exposure to things that are not wonderful. The best relationships that exist on your planet today are those that have erupted from a series of not-wonderful relationships. *Through each exposure to interacting with others, you launch continuous rockets of desires of what you prefer. And when, and only when, you are a Vibrational Match to the culmination of those desires, you will allow your rendezvous with someone who matches those intentions that you have gathered along your physical trail.*

### Sex, Art, Religion, and Monogamy

**Questioner:** I want to expand on what Jerry was saying earlier about the people in mental institutions being there because of their confusion about sex and religion. I am an artist, and I have heard it said that all great art is inspired from sex and religion; and during this discussion about sex, I realize that, from my perspective, the ultimate relationship involves a perfect fusion of creative and sexual Energy. So, regardless of what society says I should or shouldn't do in terms of my sexual choices, it feels to me that this fusion of Energies is more intense and more delicious with one person.

**Abraham:** It is true of everything. When you are positively focused in a moment, giving your attention to some positive object of attention and therefore in complete alignment with the Source within you, your Energies are aligned and your experience must be wonderful. But this is a conversation about coming into alignment with Source first, by virtue of your positive attention, not a conversation about the merits of one lover versus many.

For the most part, those who are seeking many sexual experiences are those who have not completely defined what they want. They are still collecting data, and there is nothing wrong with that.

**Questioner:** In my own mind I use the term *life partner* instead of *monogamy* to describe what I am looking for.

**Abraham:** *Life partner, for this moment,* can be a good idea. But since the details of the life you are living will always produce more clarity about what you desire, you will always be sending out new rockets of desire. The most productive and sustaining commitment that you could ever make would be to the continual aligning with the expansion that life causes you to discover.

In other words, as you live life, in all of its detail—including the person you are in love with and living with, or married to— you are still sending out rockets of desires of improvement, and the Non-Physical Source Energy part of you receives each request and melds it into the Vibrational becoming that is truly *who-you-are.* Your intention to keep up with that expansion is your true path to happiness.

Of course, those who are consistently in alignment with the Source within them would continue to inspire harmony and love from their partner. So we are not suggesting that you should not or cannot sustain a wonderful lifelong relationship with another. But we are saying that your relationship between *you* and *You* must come first, before any other relationship can remain satisfying.

Many people who are worried about the loss of love enter into marital agreements, "till death do us part" agreements, as they try to protect themselves from unwanted things. That is the opposite of what we are explaining here.

### What Is the Ultimate Sensual/Sexual Experience?

**Questioner:** What is the *sexual force?* For me, the ultimate sexual experience involves a perfect fusion with another person, communicating on all possible levels of sensual and Spiritual and emotional harmony. I feel an expansion of myself in that, like a lessening of my boundaries.

**Abraham:** Whether the sexual experience is the reason for your positive focus and therefore alignment with Source, or whether you were already in alignment with Source as you were coming into the sexual experience—it is the alignment with Source that is important.

Have you noticed that you cannot have that sort of experience if you are in the middle of an argument? You cannot be noticing flaws in your mate, or feeling insecure and incomplete in and of yourself, and have that experience.

As physical Beings, you are extensions of Source Energy, of the Energy that creates worlds; and when you take the time to consistently tune to the frequency of that Pure, Positive Energy, and then you turn your attention to your art, or to your lovemaking—you experience the Energy that creates worlds flowing through you. That is that *sexual force* that you are trying to define. . . . *A wonderful sexual experience is much more about being in alignment with your true Creative Energy Stream than it is about the actual physical interaction.*

**Questioner:** My current mate is very aware of the Non-Physical aspects of his Being. He meditates and wants to be Spiritually focused, but he says that when he engages in sexual activity, it is as if he has to become this one small physical personality and don his ego; and that, for him, he then loses that sense of the larger psychic, Non-Physical experience.

**Abraham:** In that case, he is having trouble with all aspects of physical, not just the physical sexual part. This leads us to an explanation of another flawed premise:

***Flawed Premise #20:*** *When I focus upon*
*things of a physical nature, I am less Spiritual.*

Since you are creators who have come forth from Source, you are literal extensions of Source. As you focus into this physical world, you are focusing upon creations of Source, and you are continuing to add to the creation of Source by your willingness to explore contrast and ask for continuing improvements. *Being physical does not separate you from Source, and having sex does not diminish your Spiritual connection. It is pushing against unwanted, and learning patterns of Vibration that are different from the Vibration of Source, that disconnects you from Source.*

*There is nothing more Spiritual than to allow the true spirit that is you to flow through you into your physical life. The absence of Spirituality is not about the subject or the activity. It is about the Vibrational choices that you are making.*

Source loves you, and when you do not, you are not Spiritual. Source loves the others with whom you share your planet, and when you do not, you are not Spiritual. Source understands the expanding nature of you and of *All-That-Is,* and when you think you should stand in completed perfection on every subject, you are not Spiritual. When you feel unworthy, you are not in alignment with Source.

But, as we have been discussing here, your Connection to Source must not depend upon your mate's Connection to Source. You must use you own power of focus to keep yourself in alignment with *who-you-really-are.* Your very discussion about your mate's feeling of loss of expansiveness causes the temporary loss of it within you as well.

You really cannot sort these issues out from the outside by trying to determine the rightness or wrongness of behavior. Your determination to tend to your own Connection with your own Spirituality will put you in the best position of inspiring the same in your mate. And if he continues to believe that the act of sexuality moves him away from the Spiritual person he strives to be—the *Law of Attraction* will move him out of your experience. And if you continue to remain focused upon the things that allow your alignment with your

Source—the *Law of Attraction* will bring to you another who is not only in alignment with Source as well, but who shares your values and desires regarding the subject of sexuality.

## Each Marriage Was Different but Not Better

**Questioner:** I've been married four times to two different husbands. In each case, we remarried thinking it would be better. It was different; it was not better. In each case, I can see now from what you were saying about freedom that these marriages just reinforced my desire to be free.

One of my husbands said to me, "You're really just interested in romance." And, in a sense, that was true. I thought maybe I'd rather be his mistress than his wife, because in marriage we are talking about two different things: *Sexuality* is one thing; *marriage* is another. In marriage you've got children, in-laws, property, responsibilities, duties. . . .

**Abraham:** It turns out it is not possible to separate anything from anything, though, because at the core of all of those things is you and the way you feel. As you focus upon one unpleasant or unwanted aspect of life, it bleeds over into all other aspects.

**Questioner:** That's right. And so, finally, my desire for freedom dominated so much that in each case, I left. I like the premise of life that you identify, of freedom and growth and joy, but my marriages were bringing no joy.

**Abraham:** Can you see, in looking back, that there were opportunities to look for positive aspects, but because you were fixated upon negative aspects, those became your dominant experience?

**Questioner:** Yes, but I so disliked the feeling of being hemmed in and pinned down and having to perform certain duties all the time that even though I did them, and did them well, what I wanted was to be free, to be my own person. . . .

**Abraham:** *The actual "freedom" you were seeking was freedom from negative emotion, freedom from feeling bad, freedom from not feeling good, freedom from not being* <u>*who-you-really-are.*</u>

We want you to understand that, in every moment, even those over which you feel you have no control, you have the freedom to ponder them in a way that feels better or in a way that feels worse. You have the freedom to focus upon them through the eyes of your Source or from the perspective that pinches you off from Source. Your pinned-in, not-free feelings were about your Vibrational discord, not about the subject you were focusing upon, which brought about the Vibrational discord; and that is such an important distinction.

You are not seeking freedom from experiences that cause your desires to expand, but you *are* seeking freedom from the hindering thoughts that keep you from allowing your expansion. The feeling that you are describing as being pinned in or not free is actually the feeling of not keeping up with your own expansion—the expansion, in fact, made possible by your relationship.

Have you noticed that, in terms of physical activity, you are as busy now as you have ever been? [**Questioner:** I am actually busier.] And yet you feel freer because you are no longer focused upon lack.

We are not suggesting that you should have done something differently. We are not suggesting that it was right that you stay and wrong that you go, or the other way around. But we do want you to realize that, in every moment, the way you feel is because of one thing and one thing only: the thoughts you are thinking and the Vibrational relationship with your opinion and that of the Source within you. And there is no other person, no matter how hard he tries to be a good companion, who can stand on his head in enough ways to make up for the thoughts that *you* think.

We know that some people seem to be much easier to live with than others, but, even so, we do not encourage anyone to try to guide their own behavior by trying to make others happy. *A well-meaning person who does everything in his power to make you feel better is actually making it less likely that you will direct your thoughts into harmony with your Broader Perspective. And since your feeling of freedom and joy and growth are contingent upon your Non-Physical Connection, then anything that distracts you from that important work does not help you.*

### Abraham Offers Some "Coming Together" Vows

**Questioner:** Abraham, I was involved in a religion for three years that taught that Spiritual Beings do not have physical contact, do not make love. They likened the body to a battery, and they said that by having sexual contact with another, in effect, you discharge and waste energy.

**Abraham:** The only way that you "discharge and waste energy" is by focusing upon the lack of what you desire. Since the Source within you is focused upon *who-you-really-are,* all that you have become, and all that you desire—when you focus otherwise, you lose your Connection. It is your *belief* that you are inappropriate that is causing the disharmony, not your physical behavior.

If you are having a sexual experience and you are feeling extremely guilty about it, for whatever reason, then the experience is not of value to you. Then you *are* draining your Energy. But if you are having a sexual experience and you are feeling very good about it, then the power of the Universe is behind you.

**Questioner:** Well, if only I had known 25 years ago what I have just learned here today. . . . I came from a situation where everything is a "no-no," right down to the fact that your only responsibility in life is to get married, have kids, and obey your husband. And that is even what my marriage vows said: you will love, honor, and obey this man for the rest of your life. Boy, if I had known then what I know now, I'd have run so fast.

**Abraham:** Let us offer you the perfect coming-together vows, whether you are calling them marriage or something else:

*Hello, friend. We are here as co-creators. And it is my expectation as we move forward in this marriage [or in this relationship] that both of us will find ourselves satisfied in every way that is possible. It is my desire to discover who I am and who you are. But most important to me is that I be happy so that I may inspire happiness in you.*

*I do not take your life as my responsibility. I take my life as my responsibility. And I am looking forward to a very good time here. I am anticipating that as we move forward in this life together, we will have the ultimate of all positive experiences— because that is what I intend to look for. As long as we are having a good time, let us stay together. And if we should stop having a good time, let us separate—either in thought or in physicalness— until negative do us part.*

We are not encouraging you to disassemble your marriages or your existing relationships. But we are encouraging you to tend to the relationship that matters most of all—the relationship between *you* and *You.* When you reach for thoughts about everything and everyone that harmonize with the perspective of the Source within you, you will feel the true alignment of your Being; and then, and only then, will you have something to offer another. *You must be selfish enough to be in alignment with your true self before you have anything to give.*

## PART IV

# Parenting, and the *Law of Attraction:* Creating Positive Parent/Child Relationships in a World of Contrast

## What Is the Supervising Adult's Role
## in the Child's Behavior?

If small children were allowed to interact with one another without the supervision and Vibrational interference of misaligned adults, they would naturally align to their own Broader Perspective, and they would positively interact with each other. They would observe the differences they would find in each other, but those differences would not become focal points to which they found opposition. And so, positive, effective, and pleasurable co-creation would occur. But when an adult who is not in alignment with Broader Perspective enters the picture, the positive dynamics disappear.

Many adults believe that if children are left to themselves, they will stray away from the path of rightness. And so, the adults inject themselves into the equation, watching for evidence of what they believe is wrong behavior, trying to guide the children away from what is unwanted; but children who are encouraged to focus upon "wrong" behavior, or who merely observe the adult who is now looking at them with disapproval, feel strong discord within themselves, as they are being influenced away from their loving, approving *Inner Being.*

When adults, or anyone, expect or demand that you adjust *your* behavior to something that is more pleasing to *them,* they are attempting to lure you away from the benefit of your personal *Emotional Guidance System.* And the breakdown of every relationship, the reason for every dissatisfaction, the cause of every illness or failure, stems directly from this incredible misunderstanding: *you never intended to be guided by the approval or disapproval of others, but by the harmony or disharmony of the Energies between you and your Source.*

If this group of children were to be joined by an adult who is already in alignment with her own *Source,* who is not dependent upon *their* good behavior for *her* good feeling, they would not be negatively impacted by her presence, for she would be encouraging—through the power of her example—their own personal alignment. . . . *When two or more people interact who are personally in alignment with their own Broader Perspective, the physical rendezvousing is pleasant, productive, and life-giving.*

Suddenly removing worrisome adult supervision from the experience of the children would not immediately restore them to their natural state of Well-Being, because the children have learned their Vibrational patterns from the adults, and now they are behaving with each other through the framework of those patterns. But everyone, from the oldest to the youngest among you, wants to feel good because the Non-Physical part of you, your *Inner Being, does* feel good. So, in any moment that you feel less than good, there is something very much out of alignment. . . . Because children have practiced their resistant thoughts for a shorter time than the adults who surround them, it is easier for them to return to, and maintain, their state of alignment.

## What Is a Child's Relationship with Other Children, Without Adults?

Let us remove all worrisome, guarded, controlling, resistant influences, which adults often add to the mix, from a group of children and consider what their interaction with each other would be like:

Using their physical senses, they would observe and consider one another carefully. They would see the variety of personalities and beliefs and intentions, much as you see the variety of choices at a food buffet. You do not feel threatened by the things you see that you personally do not want to eat or experience, but instead, you simply choose what you *do* prefer and put *it* on your plate.

In a similar manner, children who have not been taught to push away *unwanted* components would simply gravitate toward *wanted* components. *Children with like interests or desires, in any given point in time, would gravitate together, providing meaningful and satisfying interaction. Children with differences simply would not gravitate together—and so, a harmonious environment would result.*

Many people would argue that they have never seen such an environment, and they would be right. Others would argue that such an environment is highly unlikely, and we would agree with them, also, because it is an extremely rare child who is afforded the freedom to make his or her own choices without the deliberate influence from the adults who have fostered them into their life experience. But it is possible that once you understand your own personal *Guidance System* and how it works (that you are actually a physical extension of Non-Physical Consciousness; that your Non-Physical perspective exists even at the same time that your physical perspective exists; and that you are seeking, first and foremost, alignment with your own *Guidance System*), it is possible for you to find harmony in whatever physical environment, classroom, situation, or relationship you find yourself involved in.

By practicing your own alignment first, you could become as the children we were describing. You could interact with them, feeling no need or compulsion to push the unwanted aspects of them away. You could be (like your *Inner Being* within you) inclined to see only the best in others, as well as in yourself, therefore allowing the powerful *Law of Attraction* to match you up with only wanted things.

## What Are the Natural Father/Mother Roles?

**Jerry:** From your perspective, what is the primary, or the natural, role of a father in the progression of the lifetime of his child?

**Abraham:** The primary role of both the father and the mother is to provide an avenue for the Non-Physical Source Energy of the child to come forth into the physical experience.

**Jerry:** You don't see different roles for the father and the mother?

**Abraham:** Not different in any sense that is really important. The differences are evident when you think in terms of influences that would be offered, but parental influences are not as important as your society believes that they are. At its best, parenting provides a stable environment in the early days of adapting to this new life in this new environment and this new body. At its worst, parenting hinders the child's ability to make choices and know freedom. And so, often, parental influence is not of advantage to the child. Parents often have developed negative expectations about life, and so the influence that they offer to the child is negative, also.

### A Perspective of a Perfect Parent

**Jerry:** What is your perspective of a perfect parent?

**Abraham:** The best thing that a parent could do for a child is to understand that this child, while very small and dependent-seeming at first, is really a powerful creator who has come into this physical environment with great eagerness, purpose, and ability. The best thing a parent could do for a child is to watch for evidence of brilliance, taking note only of the positive aspects of the child. The most important benefit that any parent could offer to any child would be that of influencing the child to his own inner *Guidance System.*

We know that your intention in presenting these questions is to help guide parents to satisfying relationships with their children, and we are eager to have this discussion. But we would also like you to understand that it was not the intention of the children, coming into this time-space reality, to be born into the feathered nests of perfect parents. Once you are here, interacting with one another, experiencing the discord that often comes from interpersonal relationships, you often blame others for the way you feel or for the way your life is going. But from your Non-Physical perspective, you understand completely that the influence of those around you need not negatively impact your experience; and, in fact, not one of you, before your birth, was seeking a perfect environment in which to be born.

Most parents do want the very best for their children, and you have many varying opinions about what is the best thing to provide for your children. From our perspective, and from the perspective of your child before coming forth into this physical body, the best thing that you can offer your child is a clear example of someone who strives to align with the Source within you and to demonstrate, through the clarity of your own personal example, your effective utilization of your own *Emotional Guidance System.*

The thing that causes the most discomfort, for both parent and child, is the parent's misunderstanding of the internal wisdom and purpose of the child. And the reason why the parent misunderstands that in his child is because he misunderstands it in himself. In other words, if a parent sees a world filled with threatening, dangerous, unpleasant things and feels protective and guarded in the face of those things, he is then out of alignment with his true understanding and power. And under those conditions, he guides his child into the same guardedness.

But a parent who recognizes the value of his own *Emotional Guidance System;* who seeks alignment with his own Broader Perspective first; who understands the nature of the creative Vortex of Energy, swirling on his behalf; and whose first priority is to be in alignment with *who-he-really-is*—that parent can influence his child to seek his own Guidance.

The reason why so many people blame their parents for their failures or unhappiness is because they were trained by their parents to look to them for guidance and support. Even the most well-meaning parent cannot begin to replace the guidance and support that comes forth from within. But it is even more than that. *As each of you lives the details of the contrast that surrounds you and sends forth the constant Vibrational rockets of expansion, you must follow those rockets and allow yourself the full evolution of that expansion—or you cannot be happy.* When a parent interferes with that natural process by convincing you that what you feel is unimportant, that what your emotions are telling you should be disregarded, and that what really matters is that you comply with the opinions and rules and beliefs that are being set forth by your parents, it is no wonder that an inner rebellion occurs. And that inner rebellion will continue until the moment you deliberately and consciously come into alignment with *who-you-really-are*.

So, the best thing that a parent could do for a child is to relinquish attempted control over the child's behavior and thoughts; and to encourage the child's awareness of his own Vibrational Escrow, his Vortex of Creation, and his *Emotional Guidance System*. And the only way that a parent could influence a child's understanding of those things is by fully understanding them himself.

When a child, or a parent, feels the emptiness of *fear* or *anger* or *disappointment* or *resentment,* it is only because he is Vibrationally disallowing his Connection to the expanded Being that he has become. Those negative emotions are symptoms of his perceived loss of freedom, and the feeling of not being free is only and always about disallowing the fullness of *who-you-have-become* to be active within you in the moment.

It is interesting that the parental approach that most parents take—of observing the world, evaluating the components, deciphering the rightness and wrongness of it, sorting that into piles, and then working to guide the child away from the unwanted—is exactly contrary to the intention of both parent and child when coming into the physical experience.

And so, our perspective of a most joyous, valuable parental approach is this:

> *I understand that my child is a powerful creator who has come into this physical environment, not unlike myself, to carve out a wonderful experience. My child will have the benefit of sifting through the contrast of life in order to determine his preferences. Each time my child has an experience that amplifies his awareness of what he does not want, a Vibrational request for the improved opposite will emanate from him, and will be held for him, in his Vibrational Reality, in his Vortex of Creation. And as he pays attention to the <u>Emotional Guidance System</u>*

*within him and seeks the best-feeling thoughts he can find, he will gravitate into alignment with <u>who-he-has-become</u> and will know the fullness of <u>who-he-is.</u> And, in all of that process, he will feel the satisfaction of being the creator of his own reality. And, as his parent, I will support him completely in his becoming.*

## What Are the Familial *Inner Beings* of Parents and Children?

**Jerry:** I'd like to back up just a little bit to before we were born into this physical reality. What are the relationships between the *Inner Beings* of the parents and the child?

**Abraham:** Everyone who comes forth into the physical is an extension of Source Energy, so, in that sense, everyone is connected to everyone. And all relationships are Eternal. Once a relationship has been established, it never ceases to be. You come forth from Non-Physical in what you might call clusters of Energy or Families of Consciousness, and, without exception, you have long Vibrational Non-Physical roots with the members of your physical families.

The primary intention that you held regarding your co-creation with other people was not one of dependency at all. You knew that through the variety of interpersonal relationships, more wonderful ideas of creation would be born, and you reveled in anticipation of the new ideas that would be born from those relationships. Before the birth of the child, and even before the birth of the parent, you all anticipated your future interaction and knew the value that would come forth from it. And while you understood your Non-Physical Connection, your attention was primarily upon your expansion, and so you were not looking back, tracing roots, looking for stability and security. You were stable and secure.

**Jerry:** Is there any value to giving conscious consideration to the connection we had with our parents before we were born?

**Abraham:** There is not a great deal of value in attempting to look back at your Non-Physical origins because it is not tangible enough for you to really understand it from your physical format, and since you cannot make any real sense of it, it proves to be a distraction from what you have intended in your physical now. But, even more important, through the interactions that you have experienced together in this physical time-space reality, you have set forth powerful requests, and you are dynamic catalysts for expansion for one another. As you make an effort to align with the expanded version of yourself, you will also align with the expanded version of your parents—and the satisfaction that will come from that alignment is enormous. And you can accomplish all of that through the simple process of looking for the positive aspects of each other and finding as many reasons as possible to appreciate.

### Do Families Have Specific Prebirth Mutual Intentions?

**Jerry:** So, since our relationships are Eternal, do we have specific intentions regarding our interaction with our parents or our children after we are born? Or is it all just kind of general?

**Abraham:** In most cases, your intentions are of a general nature in the sense that you understood your creative power and the *Laws of the Universe;* and you felt eager to jump in and stir things up, experience contrast, and create. You saw your parents as a wonderful avenue into physical experience and providers of early stability while you found your creative sea legs, so to speak. Your dominant intention was to come into your physical body and immerse yourself in the contrast, which you knew would cause you to take thought and life beyond anything that it had been before. You expected your relationships with your parents, and with all other people, to provide a wonderful basis for contrast, and therefore a wonderful basis for asking, and a wonderful basis for expansions. And you knew that the details would occur through the living of life. You did not try to figure it all out in advance.

### To Whom Are We Most Responsible?

**Jerry:** Are you saying that we have no different responsibility from parent to child and child to parent than we do to any other human on the planet?

**Abraham:** We are saying that. You have come forth into this physical experience as co-creators with *everyone* upon your planet.

### What Could Parents Learn from Children?

**Jerry:** In the way that a teacher often learns from the student while the student is learning from the teacher, is it the same with parents? Do they learn from their children?

**Abraham:** When a question is born within you, the equivalent answer immediately forms in your Vibrational Reality. While you are churning in the midst of a problem, an equivalent solution forms in your Vibrational Reality. And so, it is natural that, in your interactions with one another—parent/child, teacher/student, person to person—you are discovering questions and problems that are creating answers and solutions. And so, learning (or what we prefer to call *expansion*) is the result of all co-creative experience.

**Jerry:** So, we're learning, even though we don't realize that we are?

**Abraham:** Unless you are a Vibrational Match to *who-you-really-are*—unless you are in Vibrational alignment with the expanded version of you that exists in your Vibrational Vortex—you cannot be aware of your expansion. Your expansion is constant. Keeping up with it is optional. The better you feel, the more you are keeping up with your expansion and the more you recognize that expansion. In other words, *who-you-really-are* has learned. But unless you are in the Vortex, you cannot recognize the learning. Every experience is giving you more knowledge, whether you are consciously aware of it or not.

### Why Do Siblings Respond Differently to Similar Influences?

**Jerry:** I've noticed that even though siblings are from the same set of parents, often they do not grow up as carbon copies of one another. In other words, one child can grow up to be healthy and happy and what I call a successful Being, while a brother or sister out of the same family can experience a very painful life. Does that mean that parental influence, which is similar with each child, is not a significant factor in how children turn out?

**Abraham:** It is not possible to maintain the consistent success that you refer to as *happiness* without a conscious striving for alignment with your Broader Non-Physical Being. Sometimes a parent or teacher can be a catalyst for influencing you in that direction. And everyone is born wanting to feel good and has natural instinctual tendencies toward finding that alignment. It is the influence that hinders that natural alignment that is really at the center of this discussion, because children naturally gravitate to feeling good and to their alignment with Source. In other words, if left to their own natural instincts, children would make their way more quickly into alignment. But well-meaning, guarded parents often stifle those natural impulses by worrying about what could happen, and by influencing their children away from their own *Guidance System*.

*Contrary to what most parents believe, the less concern they feel for the welfare of their child, the better off their child will be, because in the absence of the negative speculation and worry, the child is more likely to gravitate to his own alignment.*

And so, getting back to the specifics of your question . . . often the first child born to well-meaning but overprotective parents is the object of more fussing and worrying and negative influence than the children born later.

There are many factors that influence the way children, or people in general, feel, but there is only one factor of importance to consider: *does the thought being offered by this person, in this moment, harmonize with the thought of the Source within?* That is the influence you want to tune in to. All other influences are secondary. Just as a cork, when it is held down under the water, will take the most direct route back to the surface when it is released, when you release the resistance caused by your contradictory-to-Source thoughts, you will return to clarity, happiness, success, and the knowledge of your Source.

## Must Children "Take After" Their Parents?

**Jerry:** My mother used to say to me, "Well, Jerry, you know, you take after Daddy," or "You take after my father," or "your uncle," and I remember feeling strong disagreement with her.

**Abraham:** Why do you think you disagreed?

**Jerry:** I didn't necessarily think I took after anyone, but, also, it seems like when she was pointing that sort of thing out to me, it was usually because she was expressing disapproval of me at the time.

**Abraham:** That's really what we wanted you to realize. The discord you felt was because your mother's disapproving opinion activated within you a thought that was in complete disagreement with your *Inner Being*. In other words, as your mother was pointing out some flaw in you and likening it to some flaw in someone else, in a sense trying to control you by threatening you with the prospect of an unhappy outcome, your *Inner Being* was offering a very different opinion of you, to you. And your negative emotion was your indication of the disparity. That is how your *Guidance System* works. Whenever you feel negative emotion, it means that your active thought (no matter how you came upon it) does not match what your *Inner Being* knows about the subject.

**Jerry:** Even today, from time to time, something will come up that will take me back to my mother pointing out some of those flaws.

**Abraham:** And you still feel negative emotion when that happens, which means your *Inner Being* still does not agree with the words of your mother.

### Must Inherited Traits Determine My Future Experience?

**Jerry:** But aren't there traits that we pass on to our children? In the same way that physical characteristics are passed on, don't we also pass on other traits?

**Abraham:** What, specifically, are you thinking about?

**Jerry:** Like capability of mind, capability of body, abilities, health. . . . How much control does that have over me now?

**Abraham:** You need not be negatively affected by anything, but when you *are* negatively influenced, it is because you are allowing your active thought to be one that disallows what you really want.

It is quite common to pass negative *expectations* on from generation to generation, but at any point, a person who recognizes the discord of that negative thought, who recognizes that the negative emotion means that his *Inner Being* does not agree, can gradually omit those resistant thoughts, which are at the core of all illnesses, diseases, and negative experiences.

### Shouldn't Children Be Taken from "Abusive" Parents?

**Jerry:** If the current rules and regulations had been around when I was a child, and having the life that I had, I would have been taken away from my parents and put in a foster home. But at that time, I guess it was just kind of accepted as the way we were all living. And so, once I grew up and left it, I didn't look back on it as such a negative thing. I think even then I saw it more as an adventure—a way of life, with excitement and variety. And so, I never looked back and blamed my parents for how terribly I was treated. It was just the way we were all co-creating. In other words, I knew my part in it, and I assume they knew their part in it. But today, we're living in a different era, and child abuse is a big issue.

It seems to me that there are many people who deliberately expose themselves to what I would consider to be *abuse* as they play hockey or football, or face a challenger in boxing. . . . Is it possible that we are all *choosing,* and that I, in some way, chose that abusive treatment from my parents?

**Abraham:** We are appreciating your question because many people would take issue with the idea of similarity between people being beaten up by the sports they are choosing to play and children who are being beaten by their parents—but you are right about the similarity.

*What people do not understand is that you do not choose something by looking at it and shouting "Yes, I would like some of that!" You make your choices by your attention to things. In this Universe that is based on attraction, when you look at an unwanted thing, your attention to it causes an activation of the Vibration within you, and then the <u>Law of Attraction</u> brings more like it into your experience.*

Of course, it is a terrible thing when a child is abused, but it is also a terrible thing when a child is disallowed the freedom to be *who-he-really-is*. And we want you to understand that, in every case, those who are offering abuse—no matter how severe it is on your scale of things unwanted—are suffering their own disconnection from Source while offering the abuse. In other words, it is not only the child suffering the abuse from the parent that is the problem, but the adult suffering the abuse of disconnection.

Removing a child from physical abuse has to be seen as the best thing to do in that circumstance, but that action in no way solves the problem. In fact, the discord that was at the root of the abuse is only exacerbated by the physical removal of the child. Now, an unworthy-feeling parent feels more unworthy and, in an effort to feel better, usually moves to more abuse. And, often the child, who is worn down by the whole experience, feels even less secure, as he is now disallowed interaction with someone he truly loves.

The issue of child abuse will not come to an end until people understand the emotions that they feel and are able to control the direction of their thoughts. Until the self-inflicted abuse—of denying themselves Connection to *who-they-have-become,* to their *Inner Being*—subsides, violence, in all forms, will remain.

Children are resilient and return to the Connection of the Source more easily than adults do. In the absence of a social worker pointing out to you how mistreated you were, you survived the abuse, set off rockets of desire into your Vibrational Reality—and benefited from the experience. And that is the most difficult thing for people to understand. "Why would a child willingly come forth into an abusive home? Why would a loving God allow such a thing?"

*So, we remind you that you were not looking for a feathered nest, where the only thing present for you to observe was something perfect. You wanted diversity and variety, and even discord. You wanted an opportunity to define an even better experience. You knew that you were a creator, and you wanted experiences to help you to choose. You are learning and expanding all of the days of your life. Not only when you are children.*

### Without Discipline, Would Children Perform Household Chores?

**Jerry:** Abraham, where does discipline fit into the equation between parents and children? For a harmonious flow of the execution of the details of physical life—like cleaning the house, hauling out the trash, and so forth—how do you see *discipline?*

**Abraham:** We are not proponents of *discipline* because that is a component of trying to *motivate* another to action, and we never see that work out well. In other words, if a parent has a desire for a well-ordered home environment, and envisions the children living in the home as harmonious helpers, then there is no Vibrational separation within this parent, because his desires and his expectations Vibrationally match. And, under those conditions, he would *inspire* the willing cooperation from his children. We would encourage that kind of *inspiration* rather than *motivation*.

*Motivation* works more like this: A parent recognizes that there is much to be done, focuses upon children who are not helping; his observation does not match his desire, and so he experiences Vibrational discord, which feels like negative emotion. In his frustration, or anger, he issues an ultimatum about discipline that will be offered if the cooperation does not occur. The child is motivated to action because he does not want the negative consequences of his inaction. But in his lack of connection to Source, he is listless, not focused; does not do a good job; resents having to do the job; and on it goes. This is another perfect example of not being able to get there from there.

*If we were a parent, or anyone wanting to inspire positive behavior from another, we would do our personal Vibrational work first. We would align with our Source Energy by envisioning the outcome we seek and by holding those involved as positive objects of our attention. We would not allow any current unwanted behavior to be the reason for our attention to them.*

Another way of saying it is: Do not let your uncooperative children distract you from the vision of the helpful, happy children that are in your Vibrational Escrow. If you are able to hold to your vision of cooperation and not give your attention to their inaction, which disconnects you from your power, they will eventually feel the pull of your powerful influence of Connection. Your children will become very creative, actually looking for ways that they can be of benefit, rather than begrudging every little thing that they have to do because you have convinced them that if they do not do it, there will be negative consequences.

### Must "Family Harmony" Inhibit Personal Freedom?

**Jerry:** When a family is living together, whether it's a small family with one parent and one child or a larger group of 14—parents, grandparents, and children, all living in one family household—how would you suggest that they come together in an attitude of respect for one another, without losing their individual freedom? Doesn't someone have to be in charge, or can everyone be free and make their own decisions and still live in harmony as one family unit?

**Abraham:** It is possible for a group of any size to live or play or work in harmony if the individuals involved are first in alignment with *who-they-really-are*. And, it is not necessary for everyone in the group to be in alignment with their *Inner Beings* before you can experience a harmonious experience within the group. The harmony that everyone in this group dynamic is seeking is the alignment with their own *Inner Beings;* and when that is achieved, then, and only then, can harmony with other people occur. *A person who is consistently inside his own Vortex will find harmony with other people even when they are not finding harmony with him.*

*Everything that everyone desires—whether it is a material object, a physical condition, a financial situation, or a harmonious relationship— is wanted for only one reason: they believe they will feel better in having it. Once you show yourself—through practicing increasingly better-feeling thoughts, through making lists of positive aspects, by indulging in Rampages of Appreciation—that you can maintain your alignment with your own Inner Being and predominantly stay inside your Vortex of Creation, you will find harmony in the world around you, also.*

And who will be in charge? A better way of stating it is: Who will *lead* this group? And the answer to that question is: *One who is in alignment with Source is more powerful than millions who are not. And so, the person most aligned with his Inner Being, his Vortex of Creation, and the power that creates worlds will emerge as the leader. People naturally gravitate to clear-minded, stable, happy people.*

If no one in the household is in that sort of alignment, then the leadership usually falls to the biggest one or the strongest one or the loudest one. But in a group where no one is in alignment with Source, we see no real leadership.

Many people approach life and leadership in a very backward manner. They want people to behave in ways that please them so that in their observation of what pleases them, they will be pleased. We are encouraging you to focus your attention upon *thoughts* that please you, even when there is no pleasing *evidence* to observe, because a consistent absence of resistance, and of negative emotion, will cause you to align with all that is inside your Vortex. And a happy and harmonious family is in your Vortex.

## Which Family Member Should Be in Charge?

**Jerry:** So, in this family that we're discussing, isn't anyone in charge?

**Abraham:** That is like asking who is in control of the others, and the only actual control you have is over the direction of your own thought. The answer that most people would give is: "The biggest ones or the more powerful ones are in charge, or control," but your history does not bear that out, because that defies the *Law of Attraction.* One who is connected to *who-he-really-is*—in other words, one who is inside his own Vibrational Vortex—is more powerful than millions who are not.

It is not control of your family's behavior or beliefs that you seek, but control of your ability to see them as you want them to be. And when you gain control of your thoughts and are consistently in alignment with your ever-evolving, expanding version of their happy, successful lives, your power of influence will be such that others watching you will wonder what your magic is.

Our encouragement to you is that you no longer worry about what others are doing, and that you seek thoughts and words and actions that feel good to you. Train yourself into Vibrational alignment with all of the wonderful experiences and relationships that you have projected into your Vortex of Creation, and notice the harmony that will surround you as a result of your Vibrational work.

## Parents and Children, and Harmonizing vs. Traumatizing

**Jerry:** I can't help but notice how the family dynamics have changed since I was a child. My parents clearly believed that it was their responsibility to be in charge of me. I believe my mother did much of what she did out of her belief that she was doing the best thing for me, but it's obvious to me now, from what I've learned from you and because of the beatings she gave me, that she was not in alignment with her own *Inner Being* much of the time.

A short while ago, I was walking down the corridor here, and I noticed a mother and her daughter. The little girl was standing back and shouting, "No!"

And her mother said, "Oh?"

And the little girl said, "No!"

And then the mother said, "Oh, *you* want to be the leader?"

And the little girl said, "Yes." So then the pouting little girl came down the stairs while her mother waited, and proceeded to lead her mother to wherever she wanted to take her.

And I thought, *The pendulum has swung all the way in the opposite direction of when I was a child.* Today, it is not an uncommon thing to see little children making demands of their parents and to see their parents yielding to their demands. Would you discuss that, please?

**Abraham:** When neither, or none, of the people involved in a co-creative situation have taken the time to align with the power of their own Vortex so that everyone involved is outside of their Vortex, usually the one most disconnected—the one feeling the very worst—is the one who takes charge of the situation. But measuring the power of powerless people is a bit like asking a confused person for clarity. Nothing productive happens, and everyone is unhappy.

From our perspective, effective leadership or parenting or mentoring can only be offered by people who are consistently inside their creative Vortices. If you have not taken the time to align yourself with the power and clarity and knowledge of Source, you have no leadership to offer.

*Children learn their tantrums from disconnected, out-of-alignment adults.*

*Children learn their stability and clarity from adults who are in alignment with Source.*

## Must Children Be Imprinted with Their Parents' Beliefs?

**Questioner:** We often become very young parents who haven't yet learned the things that we will know later in life. How can we teach our children if *we* haven't yet learned?

**Abraham:** Often your children are still remembering things that you have forgotten: They still remember that they are good. They still expect things to turn out well for them. They are still in Vibrational alignment with their own *Inner Beings*. In other words, your children are still in their Vortices. That is one of the reasons why they are often unwilling to listen to you, or to agree with you, as you are pronouncing them inappropriate in some way. There is another important flawed premise surfacing here:

*Flawed Premise #21: It is my job as a parent to have all the answers so that I can teach those answers to my children.*

You will never have all of the answers because you will never have asked all of the questions. You will Eternally discover a new platform of contrast that will produce more questions to be answered. That, in fact, is the joy of your Eternal life . . . the joy of Eternal evolution and expansion and discovery. *Words do not teach. It is life experience that teaches. Your children did not come forth to learn from your words, but instead, they came forth to learn from their own life experiences.*

The greatest value that you can be to your children is to understand the relationship between the physical aspect of you and the Non-Physical aspect of you; to effectively utilize your own *Emotional Guidance System;* and to work, every day, to be as close as you can to your own Vortex.

If you are not inside your Vortex, and are therefore not feeling very good, do not pretend that you *do* feel good. Be real. Let your children know that you are aware that you are not in alignment with *who-you-really-are,* and demonstrate to them your desire to find that alignment. Show them the processes you have learned that cause you to feel better; and apply them often, and openly, until you are very adept at moving inside your Vortex whenever you choose.

If you pretend to be happy when you are not, or confident when you are afraid, you only cause confusion in your children. Show them, through the clarity of your deliberate example, how well your life goes when you deliberately manage the Vibrational gap between the two Vibrational aspects of you. Let them know that you *want* to feel good, and demonstrate to them that you *can* feel good whenever you choose, regardless of what is occurring around you.

And, most important of all, let your children understand that you do not hold them, or their behavior, responsible for the way you feel. Free them of the impossible bondage of needing to please you—and, in doing so, release them to their own wonderful *Guidance System.*


## Who's to Blame for This Dysfunctional Family?

**Questioner:** My childhood experience was that my parents screamed and yelled and fought, and the children were hit. I grew up with a core belief that the world was not a safe place and that really bad things could happen. And then I went into therapy for five years, and from that I came to the belief that I was not responsible for what had happened to me, but that I was a victim of two parents who were out of control.

**Abraham:** While the therapist did not want you to feel blame for what happened to you, it is really of no greater value to you to put the blame upon your parents, because whether you are feeling *blame* or *guilt,* you are still outside of your Vortex; you are still not in alignment with *who-you-are. There is no more destructive conclusion to come to than the belief that you are a victim and that others have the power to inflict pain and suffering upon you.*

Now, we know that it is difficult to understand what we are getting at when you, in fact, were the receiver of pain and suffering as a direct result of something that someone else did. And there are important factors that must be explained before this can make sense to you: Your parents did not hit you because you were bad. And your parents did not hit you because they were bad. Your parents hit you because they were out of alignment, and because they felt powerless. It is not illogical—in fact, it is extremely logical—for a person to go from a feeling of powerlessness to a feeling of *revenge* or *anger,* because that is a step toward alignment on the Vibrational Scale.

In other words, a feeling of *powerlessness* is the emotion that indicates the greatest distance from the Vortex of *who-you-really-are.* *Revenge* is closer, *anger* is closer still, *overwhelment* is closer to *who-you-really-are,* and *frustration* is much closer to *who-you-really-are. Hope* is a great deal closer to *who-you-really-are,* and now you are almost there; you are almost inside the Vortex. *Belief* in Well-Being and *knowledge* of Well-Being are inside the Vortex, along with *appreciation* and *love* and *passion* and *eagerness* and all good-feeling emotions.

As you found yourself in the middle of a terrible and uncontrollable situation, your response was to be afraid. And as you cowered and cried (an absolutely understandable response), you evoked more of what you did not want from your parents. It may be hard to understand, but if you could have mentally removed yourself from the drama of those battles, focusing upon your toys, staying in your room, not becoming a part of the Vibrational mix of it, your parents would have left you out of the drama. But it is not an easy thing not to notice what is going on or have an emotional response to it.

The same thing was true of your parents. Undoubtedly there were unwanted things going on in their lives that they had a difficult time ignoring, which caused them to be pulled into more and more unwanted situations. It is a sort of chain-of-pain that develops as someone is unhappy (and often justifiably so), so he or she lashes out at another, who lashes out at another, who lashes out at another. . . .

Most people involved in the chain-of-pain, whether they are children or adults, come to the conclusion, from the uncomfortable life that they are living, that they are not worthy and that good things do not come to them. And because they feel that way—that is what happens.

And then, most, even those in therapy, spend a great deal of time trying to sort out the rightness or the wrongness of the behaviors of the parties involved. Children blame themselves, children blame their parents, parents blame themselves, parents blame their children, and on and on the chain-of-pain goes.

Only when you are willing to find a thought, any thought, that brings you a feeling of relief can you begin your trek up the *Emotional Scale* in the direction of the *love* and *appreciation* that represents *who-you-really-are*. And only from inside the Vortex can you fully appreciate the experience and the expansion, and the understanding, that it has given you.

Most people believe that what they are looking for is someone to love them, and they also believe that it is the responsibility of their parents to love them. But parents in *despair,* far from their Vortices of Well-Being, have no love to give. And so, the child assumes he is not loved because something is wrong with him, rather than understanding he is not being loved by his parents because they are out of alignment with love.

Again, we must say that humans are looking for love in all the wrong places. Look to your Vortex; look to the expanded you; look to your Source; look to the resource of Love. It is always there for you, but you must find Vibrational alignment with it, within you. You must tune your Vibrational frequency to that of love—and your Vortex will envelop you—and you will be surrounded by love.

### But How Could Babies "Attract" Unwanted Experiences?

**Questioner:** But how do you attract terrible experiences when you are only nine months old?

**Abraham:** Even though you are only nine months old in your physical body, you are a very old and wise creator focused in that baby's body. And you came with powerful intentions to experience contrast and to launch clear rockets of desire into your Vibrational Reality for the purpose of expansion.

*People often assume that because a child is not yet offering words, the child could not be the creator of its own experience, but it is our promise to you that no one else is creating your experience. Children emanate Vibrations—which are the reason for what they attract—even from their time of birth.*

Most children are born into situations that do not challenge their natural tendency to remain aligned with their own Vortices. Most children are not influenced out of their Vortices by those who surround them in the early days of their physical experience. But sometimes, when you have come into the physical experience with a powerful intention to teach Well-Being, you intended, even before your birth, to have early exposure to contrast that would stimulate your desire early on in your physical experience, because you understood the power of the asking that would come out of that experience. When you really know what you *do not* want, you ask with greater clarity for what you *do* want—and your Vortex expands more rapidly as a result.

You also understand, from your Non-Physical perspective before your birth, that the true source of discomfort or negative emotion or sickness or all things unwanted, is misalignment with your Vortex, misalignment with *who-you-really-are.* And so, there is actually an eagerness on the part of all Beings coming into physical bodies to have early contrasting experiences in order to project rockets of desire to their Vortices of Creation, because the more powerfully the Vortex spins, the louder the call of Source. *All Non-Physical Beings understand that when wanting is higher, awareness of resistance is greater; and so, since resistance is the only thing that ever thwarts joyous creation, then the greater the awareness, the better.*

We understand that if you are still standing outside of your Vortex, disconnected from the powerful Being that has emerged from the contrast that you have lived, none of this explanation will be satisfying. But it is our promise to you that as you look for more reasons to feel good; as you try to give your parents, or anyone who has hurt you or betrayed you, the benefit of the doubt; as you move into your Vortex, you will then understand. For when you merge with the evolved, expanded part of you, surrounded by the

Vibrational equivalent of everything that you have been asking for and that you have Vibrationally become—you will harbor no ill will toward anyone who helped you achieve that. In fact, you will stand in appreciation for the part they played in your joyous expansion.

## Why Are Some Children Born Autistic?

**Jerry:** What would cause a child to be born with an unwanted physical condition? For instance, there seems to be an almost epidemic number of children being born with the condition called *autism.* At what point before its birth could a baby be thinking thoughts of lack?

**Abraham:** From your physical perspective, you often do not remember the immense value of contrast and difference, while from your Non-Physical perspective before your birth, it is often a very big factor in the choices that you make. Many parents and teachers who have forgotten the value of contrast and differences have a powerful desire that their children "fit in," which has resulted in a truly troubling epidemic of conformity. And so, many Beings come into the physical experience with an express intention of being different enough that they cannot be controlled into conformity. All Non-Physical Beings coming forth into the physical experience are clear and eager and sure, and they never come from a position of lack. No exceptions.

# PART V

# Self-Appreciation, and the *Law of Attraction:* Appreciation, the "Magical" Key to Your Vortex

## Appreciation, Your Key to the Vortex

We have very much enjoyed our interaction with you in presenting our knowledge of the Universe, of the *Laws of the Universe,* and of the important part that you play. Always, our primary intention as we interact with our physical human friends is to help you remember who you actually are so that you may experience the fullness of the appreciation for your part in this joyous, Eternal, Universal creation.

*It is an important dance that we dance with one another as we dialogue back and forth between physical perspective and Non-Physical perspective, because both perspectives are integral to the whole. Both the perspectives of physical and of Non-Physical are essential to our Eternal expansion, but the most significant understanding that we are presenting in this book, and the most important knowledge that you will ever acquire, is about the integration of those two Vibrational vantage points.*

Your physical viewpoint is spectacularly compelling to you as you explore it and observe it through the detailed deciphering of your physical senses. The contrast of your tactile, sensuous, fragrant Earth environment, in all of its detail and vividness, causes you to pronounce your world "reality." Indeed, your attention to your physical world is serving you and *All-That-Is* extremely well, but there is more to the picture and more to the story of reality than what you are discovering with your physical senses here on your amazing planet, in your amazing galaxy, in your amazing time-space reality. For all of this, all that you see, is a precursor to that which is to come: a bouncing-off place to more joyous reality and more joyous becoming.

When people observe the wonder of their galaxy and planet and speculate that it was somehow set into motion by Non-Physical forces, while their understanding and explanations are scanty, they are essentially accurate: *Your physical world is an extension of Non-Physical Energy and creation. Everything that you now behold was created from the conscious attention of Source Energy.*

The story of the creation of you and your world is not a story of something that happened—but a story of something that *is* happening. The Source Energy that created your world continues to flow forth to you and through you for the continuation of creation and for the expansion of the Universe.

Often, humans, in their humility, refuse to accept their important role in the continuing expansion of *All-That-Is,* and that is the reason why we are offering this book. It is our desire to awaken within you the memory of *who-you-really-are* and of why you are here. We want to help you return to the knowledge of your creative ability; we want you to reap the benefits of the important work you are doing in your physical bodies; we want you to return to the Vortex.

Your physical exposure to your physical world is providing the contrast that is necessary for you to form your opinions and desires about how life could be improved. And even though you cannot see them, and are often unaware of them, your desires for improvement shoot out from you as Vibrational rockets, or messengers of request. They shoot out into the Vibrational atmosphere in the same way that the original rockets that created your planet were sent; and they are received by the Source of the Energy that creates worlds, the same Source Energy that is the origin of *All-That-Is.* And those ideas, requests, and desires are understood; and—in the moment of their launch—they are answered.

Most people have neither an awareness of the launching of the rockets nor of the receiving and answering by Source, but even so, powerful new creation is begun. Some people, as they contemplate these words, can understand the logic in the Eternal nature of creation. Many can accept that creative forces still exist, and that expansion still continues. But the part that is most often misunderstood, or overlooked, by our human friends is that, in the living of physical life and in the launching of those rockets of desired expansion, it is not only an expanded world you are creating—it is an expanded you.

As you observe sickness, in yourself or in another, you set forth a new Vibrational request for wellness that is received and answered by Source. When the contrast of your physical world reveals to you corruption or injustice, you set forth a new Vibrational request for fairness and justice. When someone is rude to you, your rocket asks for nicer experiences. When you do not have enough financial resources, your rocket asks for more. And with each request offered all day, every day, a Vibrational Escrow, or Vibration Reality, is forming. The Broader Non-Physical part of you, the part of you that existed even before your birth, the part of you that exists in the Non-Physical even while you are focused in physical—the Source within you (your *Inner Being*)—not only answers your request for improvement, but becomes it.

People often have a difficult time conceptualizing a creator, or a force, or the process through which something as amazing as your planet, spinning in its orbit in perfect proximity to other planets, could have come to be. And yet, even though you do not understand it, and cannot begin to explain it, you are—every one of you—continuing to add to the expansion of all of that through your living of life and the launching of rockets into the Vibrational Reality that will someday be fully realized by physical inhabitants.

We have written this book because we want to call your attention to the Vibrational Reality that you are in the process of creating. We want you to be aware of your Vortex of Creation; and most important of all, we want you to find a way, by the deliberate directing of your own conscious thought, to become a Vibrational Match to the contents of your swirling Vibrational Vortex of Creation, because every desire that has been born within you thus far exists there, just as you have dreamed it to be, waiting for your alignment.

Everything that you see that is now physical, tangible, visible, audible *reality* was previously swirling in a Vibrational Vortex of Creation; for first there is *thought,* then *thought-form,* then *reality* as you know it in your physical world. Your dreams and desires and ideas of improvement have been received by the Broader part of you; and as that older, larger, wiser part of you focuses purely upon your requests, holding no resistance whatsoever, the powerful *Law of Attraction* responds. And then, all cooperative components (all components with same Vibrational frequency) are drawn into this swirling Vibrational Reality, this precursor to the physical reality that is now available to you. Only one thing is necessary for this Vibrational Reality to become real in a physical sense, manifested into things and experiences that you can see and hear and smell and taste and touch: *you have to go into the Vortex!*

When your husband, in his frustration, yells at you, and you are reeling in the absence of love that he is currently showing you, you launch a rocket of desire to be respected, to be loved; for a mate who feels better, for a mate who loves you. And *click, click, click, click,* those requests are received and integrated into your Vibrational Vortex of Creation. And now, the *Law of Attraction* responds to this swirling creation, drawing in all cooperative components—and your newly amended creative Vortex expands. But there is a very important question that you may want to consider: *Are you, right now, a cooperative component? Are you in the Vortex?*

- If you are still reeling in discomfort from your mate's verbal abuse—you are not in the Vortex.

- If you are telling your girlfriend about what happened, defending your innocence in the whole affair—you are not in the Vortex.

- If you are longing for the time when he treated you better—you are not in the Vortex.

- If you are letting it go and remembering how you felt when you decided to marry him—you are in the Vortex.

- If you are not taking his outburst personally and are focused upon other positive aspects of your experience—you are in the Vortex.

- If you feel terrible—you are not in the Vortex.

- If you feel better—you are closer to the Vortex.

A simple way to understand the Vortex is this:

- Before your birth into this physical body, you were in the Vortex (no resistant thought resides there).

- A part of the Consciousness that was you is now focused into the physical you that you know as *you.*

- The contrast of your life causes you to send rockets of expansion into your Vortex, where the larger Non-Physical part of you exists.

- The Vortex, which holds only your positive requests for improvement and expansion, holds no thoughts that contradict improvement and expansion.

- The *Law of Attraction* responds to the pure, nonresistant Vibration of your Vortex and gathers all cooperative, Vibrational-matching components that are necessary for the completion of the creation.

- You are one of the components of your creation.

- In fact, *you are the creation.*

- So the only question is: *Are you, from your physical format, right now, a Vibrational Match to your creation?* Or not?

- And the way you feel, right now, as you focus upon the subject of creation is your answer.

- If you are angry—you are not a Vibrational Match—and you are not in the Vortex.

- If you are feeling appreciation—you are a Vibrational Match—and you are in the Vortex.

*The key to getting inside your Vibrational Vortex of Creation, of experiencing the absolute absence of resistance, of achieving complete alignment with all that you have become and all that you desire, and of bringing to your physical experience everything that you desire—is being in the state of appreciation. And there is no more important object of attention to which you must flow your appreciation than that of self.*

*The habit of thought, or belief, that holds most people outside of their Vortex of Creation, more than all other thoughts put together, is the lack of appreciation of self.*

## Why Would Someone Lose Self-Confidence?

**Jerry:** Well, I guess I usually talk about my own experiences because they are the ones where I'm surest about what happened and how I felt. I remember that, as a little child, I had such self-confidence. I didn't know a stranger. I felt capable of accomplishing just about anything. But then, as the years went by, I began to accept the criticism of others, I began to feel criticism toward myself, and I lost that self-confidence. I became almost introverted.

Today, when I see little children coming in with that bravado and high self-confidence, I remember feeling that way. But then, little by little, I see them get what I call "chopped down" as their self-confidence diminishes. Would you clarify why we experience this erosion of self-appreciation and how we can prevent it? And how can we uplift others to a higher degree of self-appreciation?

**Abraham:** You are right—it is really only through your own experiences that you can understand anything, for this reason: Your life has caused you to expand, to launch rockets into your Vibrational Vortex of Creation; but true knowledge, or understanding, is experienced only when you allow yourself to catch up with and merge with those rockets. No knowledge is ever experienced by your trying to catch up with rockets that have been launched by others. That is why words do not teach. It is only your own life experience that teaches.

That is why you are so fiercely independent in the beginning: not wanting to take other people's word for things, wanting your own experience, wanting to make your own decisions, wanting your own freedom to choose. None of that wanting ever recedes or becomes less. In fact, it becomes more! *The reason why the bravado that you are born with usually fades is because you allow yourself to become distracted from your Vortex. In other words, you allow others to convince you that it is more important to you to pay attention to how they feel than how you feel.*

Every emotion that you feel is an indication of your relationship with your Vortex. When you feel confident, that means that your current thought is a perfect match to the way the Source within you, from inside your Vortex of Creation, is feeling about you. When you feel embarrassed, that means that your current thought does not match the way the Source within you is feeling about you. So, when parents or teachers or friends project an attitude of disapproval toward you (in an effort to evoke a more-pleasing-to-them behavior from you), if you respond to their disapproval by modifying your thoughts, words, or behavior to please them, you have distracted yourself from your own true Guidance and from your own true Source of confidence.

And so, it is not that your self-confidence *erodes,* but rather that you are disallowing the continual replenishment of it. As you seek approval from them, you are distracted from your fountain of Source Energy renewal. Again, "looking for love in all the wrong places."

For you to uplift others, you must direct them to their own fountain of replenishment. You do not help them by asking them to respond to your approval or disapproval. Many of you think that the way to uplift others is by showering them with your own approval. But if they are looking to you for the refreshment of their being and you have other things to which you want to give your attention, they will be in trouble. Or if they are looking to you and you yourself are not connected to your own Stream of replenishment, so you have nothing to give them, they are again in trouble. But if you help them understand that they have a Source of refreshment that is independent of all other humans, and that they have only to understand the nature of their own Vortex of Creation and align with it often, now you have offered them true upliftment that will serve them, independently, all of the days of their lives.

## What Is a First Step Toward Self-Appreciation?

**Jerry:** I recall the negatives that were directed at me, criticizing me and causing me to feel really bad about myself, but then I remember my grandfather, who uplifted me tremendously. There were teachers who deflated me and tried to humble me and embarrass me and belittle me, but then I remember my speech teacher, Mr. Hanley, who uplifted me and made me feel good about myself. I remember the people in the gymnasium who made fun of me, but then Mr. Piers, the gym coach, uplifted me tremendously. I remember enjoying participating in the teenage programs at the church and in the choir and the Scouts, but then there was so much criticism in the church directed at all other churches and toward the rest of the world that I just wanted to get away from it. I wanted to take my physical body away.

But now, what I am hearing from you is that it's not an action kind of thing—that we need to leave what we don't want. We don't need to look to those other teachers or family members to uplift us or give us self-confidence, although it does help. We can find it directly in ourselves, no matter what's going on around us, right?

**Abraham:** You have just pointed out, through the examples in your own life, the problem with looking to others for your upliftment. Those who were in a state of appreciation—and therefore were in alignment with Source; with their Vortex; with the Pure, Positive Energy that creates worlds—as *they* held you as your object of attention, you felt the *advantage* of their gaze. But when those not in their Vortex, not in alignment with Source, held you as the object of their lackful attention, you felt the *disadvantage* of their gaze. It is the inconsistency of the responses that you garner from others that eventually erodes your confidence.

Your Vortex of Creation, the Source within you (your *Inner Being*), is undeviating and dependable. When you make your way to your Vortex of Creation through the thoughts that you choose—you will always be replenished. A balanced, good-feeling life requires that you return often to drink from the Source.

## How Does the *Law of Attraction* Affect Competition?

**Jerry:** Do you see competition as helpful or unhelpful? When I was a teenager, whenever I saw someone doing a spectacular dive on a diving board, I felt inspired to come up with something even better. Or if I'd see a juggler who could outdo me in some way, then I'd try to develop juggling routines that no one else had done. It seemed to me that I was constantly evaluating myself in comparison with someone else's talent and ability. But then, as an adult, I tried to pull myself away from anything that felt competitive, because I didn't like the idea that in order for someone to win, someone else had to lose. I liked winning, but I didn't like losing; and I didn't really enjoy others' losing, even when I was winning.

**Abraham:** You have deliberately positioned yourself in this time-space reality filled with variety and contrast because you enjoy the stimulation of thought that it provides. The key to effectively utilizing the variety or competition of ideas and experiences that surrounds you is to use it to stimulate your desire, but then once your desire has been formulated and your rockets have been launched into your Vortex, to now turn your undivided attention to you and your thought-by-thought relationship with your own Vortex. Once your rockets have been launched, the physical competition has served its purpose for you. In other words, competition is a tremendous impetus to *Step One* of your Creative Process, but it is a tremendous hindrance to *Step Three* of your Creative Process.

**Jerry:** Aren't you speaking more of comparison than competition?

**Abraham:** Competition is just an advanced version of comparison. And it is important to remember that there is never an ending to the game, for there will always be another combination of contrast that will cause you to launch another rocket of desire. Therefore, you will always have the fun of moving toward your Vortex; of closing the Vibrational gap; and of experiencing, in detail, your newly launched expansion.

## What about Comparing Ourselves Unfavorably to Others?

**Jerry:** Long after I was able to afford a more luxurious car, I continued to drive more conservative cars because I remembered being critical of people who drove luxury cars. Then once I left my criticism of luxury-car owners behind, I drove the most expensive car that was made. But, in both cases, I was influenced by the response that I would attract from other people. Would you call that an unhealthy game?

**Abraham:** Anytime what someone else thinks about you becomes more important than your own balance with self, you are in a less-than-healthy position. Anytime you take action to try to manipulate or affect others' opinions or attitudes toward you, you are in a less-than-healthy position, because you are replacing your own *Guidance System* with their *opinion*.

## What If We're Fearing a Worldwide Financial Crisis?

Most people are so distracted by what others are doing and what others are thinking that they forget to tune themselves to their own expansion. And when the resulting empty feeling comes, they incorrectly assume that it has something to do with the behavior or opinions of the others. But it is never about that. *Every emotion that you feel, good or bad, is about the relationship between your current thought and the understanding of the Source within you on the same topic.*

Some people are feeling acute fear or anxiety because they are personally, right now, without work or income. But the fear that *most* people are feeling today is because of their negative speculation about how bad conditions may yet become and the negative impact that those future, unwanted conditions may have on their personal lives.

By giving attention to the financial trauma that some people are experiencing, and by adding to that trauma with their own anticipation of how much worse it *could* become—without meaning to, and certainly without wanting to, people are adding massively to an even worsening economic situation. Their worried thoughts are not a driving negative force that is somehow destroying businesses and employment and resources, but those thoughts are holding *them* apart from the financial well-being that they so much desire.

When you see others experiencing hardship and become fearful that similar hardship will befall you, you hold yourself in a Vibrational tension that disallows your natural Well-Being from flowing. *As more people observe hardship and strike a tense, resistant pose—and therefore disallow their own Well-Being—others use them as their reason to do the same. And, in a very short time, a very negative pattern of resistance can sweep through your population. The good news in this scenario is that, in every moment that every person is feeling negative emotion about the economic state, Vibrational requests for more abundance are launched—and those requests are heard clearly, and responded to immediately, by Source. And a Non-Physical, Vibrational Vortex of Creation begins to swirl in powerful response to that powerful asking—and all compatible components are drawn into the Vortex for the discovery and relief of those who allow themselves to be drawn inside.*

Although there is a great deal of confusion about what to do about the economic situation of your nation, or of your world, your solution does not lie in the action you take, but in the Vibrational stance that you discover that allows you to see clearly the path to the solutions that you seek. In simple terms, since the solutions you seek have already been assembled by the powerful *Law of Attraction* inside the Vibrational Vortex of Creation, you have only to stop harboring the thoughts that hold you outside of the Vortex, for by often offering thoughts upon a subject that are Vibrationally opposite in nature, you prevent yourself from finding the solutions you seek.

The personal and collective *contradictions* in thoughts regarding abundance and financial well-being are running rampant in your society, in your government, in the minds of those who propose to resolve the situation, and in the general public at large. In other words, you cannot have it both ways: Your businesses acknowledge that they want people to buy their products and services, and to spend money to stimulate the economy; and they acknowledge that many thriving businesses make for a general thriving economy. But then a contradictory assertion also rings out that says it is arrogant and improper to display your opulence by spending too much money or living too well.

Many people want to experience more personal wealth at the same time that they are criticizing those who are already experiencing personal wealth:

- "We need you to spend/Your spending makes us uncomfortable."

- "I want to be wealthy/Wealthy people are somehow immoral."

- "I would like to be rich/Rich people are depriving poor people of resources."

- "Spending stimulates the economy/Spending is wasteful."

- "Spend, and stimulate the economy/Save and sacrifice for the sake of the economy."

- "I want to thrive/There is not enough to go around."

*It is natural that you thrive, and the resources are there for all to thrive. But chronic thoughts of shortage, or chronic thoughts of pushing against those who are thriving, hold you in contradiction to your own desires and, more important, to what you have put into your Vortex of Creation for yourself.*

The negative emotion that you feel when you believe that others are depriving you of something is not about what *they have* and therefore what *you do not have*. Your negative emotion, in every case, is about what you are, in the moment of your negative emotion, depriving yourself of receiving. And, even more important, if you had not already called forth the abundance by virtue of what you have been living, and if the abundance you have asked for were not already swirling in your Vortex in anticipation of your receipt of it, you would not feel negative emotion as you deprive yourself of it.

*If you seek financial well-being for yourself—you must praise it wherever you see it.*

*If you would like more abundance for yourself, personally, or for others you care about—you must not criticize those who are experiencing abundance. When you criticize or condemn or push against anything, you activate an opposing Vibration to what you seek. Every time. No exceptions.* Which leads us to another flawed premise:

**Flawed Premise #22:** *I can criticize successful people and still achieve my own success.*

*Whenever you criticize, or push against, anything, you hold yourself outside of your Vortex. Your own success can only be realized when you are inside your Vortex. Flawed premises hold people outside of their Vortices of abundance and prevent them from the ease and Well-Being that they deserve. You cannot "criticize yourself" to success. You cannot "condemn yourself" to Well-Being. The negative emotion you feel, in your disappointment, anger, and condemnation, is the indication of the opposing thoughts within you. You are opposing your success. You are opposing your abundance. You are opposing your alignment with Source. You are opposing the Vortex that holds all that you seek.*

### Selfishness, and the *Law of Attraction?*

Some offer criticism because we place such emphasis on the value of your feeling good, accusing us of teaching *selfishness.* And we acknowledge that true selfishness is at the very core of our teaching, because if you are not selfish enough, if you do not care how you feel, if you are not willing to continually redirect your thoughts in the direction of feeling good, you cannot come into alignment with the Source within you. And unless you are in alignment with the Source within you, you have nothing to give another. Alignment with Source—being inside your Vortex of Creation, becoming one with the true expanded version of you—is the ultimate selfishness.

And yes, in that state of alignment, all good things must come to you. Every rocket of desire that you have launched will be fulfilled.

*True success is not the attainment of things, or the achievement of tasks, or the achievement of financial abundance. True success is the coming into alignment with You. Yes, selfishly aligning with your desires, your clarity, your confidence, your knowledge, your love—with Yourself!*

## Must We Be Guided by the Intentions of Others?

**Jerry:** If each of us felt totally at one with ourselves, if we were consistently inside the Vortex, would there be any need for leaders or people in the world to control us or to tell us what to do?

**Abraham:** Your alignment with Source is so much more than any guidance you could ever receive from any other place. Sometimes, as an individual or as a culture, you have the benefit of a leader who is leading from *inside* the Vortex. And when that happens, you feel the power of the individual, and you often receive clarity and insight when you listen. But, more often, as a leader begins to lead, as he focuses upon the problems to be solved, he moves *outside* the Vortex and then attempts to lead from his vastly weakened position. If we were standing in your physical shoes, we would not seek a leader, asking him to go into the Vortex in order to lead you. We would find our own way in, and we would work to consistently stay there, and we would discover the power that creates worlds flowing through our own fingertips.

Most often, you gather together in numbers out of your feeling of weakness. From your places of insecurity, you try to make it better. But a large gathering of people who are not in their Vortices never offers clarity or strength or solutions. *One person consistently inside the Vortex is more powerful than millions who are not.*

## How Can I Feel More Self-Appreciation?

**Jerry:** Well, this philosophy clearly is about the value of our feeling good. Can you guide us on how to feel good? Can you give us a process or a technique to feel good about ourselves? In other words, speak to us about how we can deliberately acquire self-appreciation.

**Abraham:** The ultimate in self-appreciation is the allowing of yourself to be in Vibrational alignment with Source, with the expanded you inside your Vortex, and it is not necessary that you focus upon yourself in order to do that. In fact, for most people, especially in the beginning, it is easier for you to find alignment while focusing on many other things, other than you.

Over time, you have developed many opinions and attitudes, and habits of thoughts—or beliefs about yourself—that when activated hold you outside the Vortex. And so, it is easier to get inside the Vortex by focusing upon other subjects that are easier for you to feel good about.

For example, you could think about your favorite pet, and in your appreciation of that pet, you may move right into the Vortex because you do not hold resistant thoughts of envy or blame or guilt toward your pet. We would really like you to see that when you are thinking about your cat—or anything that holds no resistance to your Vortex, and so you flow easily inside—you are then joined (or better stated, you have *allowed* yourself to merge) with the whole of that which you are. We would call that the ultimate self-appreciation, even though you were not thinking about *you* in order to accomplish it. If we were standing in your physical shoes, we would choose the subjects that we easily feel good about as our focal points for getting into the Vortex.

Your physical orientation has trained you to be objective, to weigh the pros and the cons of every subject, but you will discover, as you play the game, that the pros of a subject may very well put you right inside the Vortex; while, as you focus upon the cons, the Vortex will spit you right out. *You cannot focus upon unwanted and be in the Vortex at the same time. . . .* By often making the statement "Nothing is more important than that I feel good," you will make yourself more aware of your proximity to your Vortex.

## What Is My Purpose for Life?

As people stand amidst the contrast of their physical lives, they often wonder, *What is my purpose for life? Why am I here?* And we want you to know that you deliberately came to enjoy your exploration of the contrast of your time-space reality because you knew that it would inspire new ideas and desires, and that it was, in fact, the foundation for expansion.

It is our expectation that, through the reading of this book, you now have a clearer understanding of how you, in your physical body, fit into the larger picture of creation and the important role you play, from your physical format, in that larger picture.

We are most eager about helping you remember that even though you are powerfully focused into your physical body, in your physical reality at this time, you—and we—are creating a Vibrational Reality that holds the promise of your future manifestations. And the amount of time that will expire before *you* begin to see and experience those desired manifestations is only the amount of time that it takes you to get into your Vortex. In other words, your moods and attitudes and emotions are your indicators of your proximity to your Vortex, to your Vibrational Reality, to everything that you desire, and to all that you have become.

If you have been a student of our teachings for any length of time, or have read the series of books that have preceded this one, you have discovered that we are prolific spewers of processes, and we want you to know that every process that we offer is done so with the intention of helping you release any resistance that is holding you outside of your Vortex.

As we conclude this book, we are going to offer a handful of very simple processes that, if consistently applied, will help you achieve a gradual but steady alignment with the *Energy-that-is-really-you,* and will assure your entry into your Vortex; and once you are consistently there—your physical life will be transformed.

## Some Processes to Get into the Vortex

It is not necessary to deliberately apply these, or any, processes in order to raise your Vibration and get into the Vortex. Many people move easily into the Vortex simply because they like feeling good and consistently offer thoughts that do feel good. You could know nothing about what we are offering here in this book; you could be completely unaware of the *Law of Attraction,* know nothing about the Three-Step Creative Process, be unaware that you are an extension of Source Energy . . . and still be consistently inside the Vortex—simply because you like feeling good, and so you direct your thoughts to what does feel good. Your grandmother could have offered an example of a cheerful person who looks for the best in everyone and everything, and since you felt the power of her influence of Connection, you may very well be doing the same thing. But if you are like most people who are observing the world around you, you have probably developed patterns of thought that do not serve you, and that hold you—while you may be unaware of it—outside the Vortex.

When you have a belief about something (a belief is only a thought you keep thinking) and you think about it often, and therefore keep it active in your Vibration, the *Law of Attraction* simply brings you evidence to support it (because you get what you think about, whether it is something that you want or something that you do not want). And without making a decision to do something about changing the pattern of Vibration that is contained within those beliefs, nothing can change in your experience, and you will have no deliberate control of your proximity to your Vortex or to *who-you-have-become* and what you desire.

And so, the following processes are offered to help you release resistance and to provide an inevitable path into your Vortex:

### A *Bedtime-Visualization Process*

Tonight, as you lie in your bed, focus your attention on the best-feeling things you can find. Draw your thoughts inward, away from any overwhelming details of your day, and feel the ease that occurs when you focus up close to where you are. Think, in detail, about your bed: its comfort, the feel of the bedding. Think about the relationship of your body to the mattress, and imagine the mattress floating or your body being absorbed into it. . . . Relax and breathe, and enjoy the comfort of your bed. Say things such as: *I like this. This is a good thing. I have a good life.* And sleep.

### When You Find Yourself Awake

When you awaken in the morning, deliberately stay in your bed with your eyes closed for five minutes or so, with the intention of basking in the most pleasant things you can bring to mind. . . . During your slumber, you have released all resistance, and if you do not activate it now, it will not come up. So this extra five minutes in bed is for the purpose of allowing your naturally higher Vibration to get a strong foothold. . . . Find pleasure in your thoughts, and hold them in that pleasant place as long as possible. And, in the moment that the slightest uneasiness surfaces, breathe deeply, focus back upon the comfort of your bed, find something to appreciate— and then get up to begin your day.

### The *Focus-Wheel Process*

Once you have eaten your breakfast and refreshed your body, sit in a comfortable place with the intention of doing one or two *Focus Wheels,* a process that has been designed specifically to help you release resistance and focus you into your Vortex. And, in fact, the process itself mimics a swirling, attracting Vortex, which gathers momentum as it swirls.

Have you seen the hand-pushed merry-go-rounds that are often in school or park playgrounds? It is common to see children piling on and then making the merry-go-round go faster and faster. It is easy to get onto it when it is stopped or going slowly, but when it is really going fast, it is harder, or impossible, to jump on. And if you try, the momentum of the wheel tosses you off in the bushes. Considering this merry-go-round will help you understand the *Focus-Wheel Process*.

During the course of your normal day, you will come across many things that, as you see them or remember them, will cause an activation of resistance within you. It may be some unpleasant thing you read about in the newspaper, or something that someone says to you; but when resistance occurs, you will always feel the pang of negative emotion. Often you cannot stop what you are doing right then to deal with newly activated resistant thought, but we do encourage you to make a mental—or better still, written—note about it: *My employer's attitude toward me makes me uncomfortable. He doesn't appreciate the contribution that I make here.* Now you have a subject for tomorrow's *Focus Wheel* segment.

So yesterday, while lying in bed, you released resistance before sleeping. During the night, you released all resistance. And when you awakened, you deliberately kept the resistance-free zone going by basking for a while. You had breakfast and showered and brushed your teeth, and now you plan to sit for 15 or 20 minutes to clean up any pieces of resistance that are lurking in your thought processes. And the very best time to do that is while you are feeling good.

As you read your note about your perception of your employer's attitude toward you, you will reactivate the resistant thought. So, take a large sheet of paper and write at the top of it: *My employer's attitude toward me makes me uncomfortable. He doesn't appreciate the contribution that I make to his business.*

Now draw a large circle on the page, as large as the page will allow. Then draw a small circle in the center of that large circle, and then draw 12 small circles around the perimeter of the large circle, positioning them like the numbers on the face of a clock.

Whenever something happens in life that points out to you, with great clarity, something that you do not want, an equally clear awareness of what you do want hatches within your awareness at the same time. By focusing upon your belief that your employer does not appreciate the contribution that you make, an equal *desire* is born: *I like it when my employer understands the depth of my interest and the contribution I make to the success we are all having here.* Write a version of that inside the circle in the center of the wheel.

Now, like the merry-go-round in the playground, you must find a way to get on the wheel. If your resistant thoughts are spinning too fast, you will not be able to get on. The wheel will just toss you off in the bushes. So try to find something that you already believe that matches, in some ways, what you felt when you wrote the words in the center circle.

You may think:

- *My boss does appreciate me.* (Off in the bushes.) You really do not believe that—not right now, anyway.

- *My boss doesn't deserve me.* (Now you are not even trying.)

Keep focusing back on the words in the center of your *Focus Wheel.* It will help you to feel the activation of beliefs that you already hold that match that sentiment.

- *My boss wants his company to succeed.* (You are on the wheel.) Write that at the 12 o'clock spot on your wheel.

- *His company was well under way when I joined.* (You have not solved any problem here, but this statement is something that you believe, and it does somehow make you feel better.) Write that at the 1 o'clock spot on your wheel.

- *There are aspects of this work that I really enjoy.* (That is true, too, and now you are gaining a bit of momentum.) Write that at the 2 o'clock spot on your wheel.

- *I really enjoy it when my boss and I are clicking.* (That is true, and it feels good.) 3 o'clock spot.

- *We both can feel the synergy of our collaboration.* (More momentum . . . now you're rolling.) Write that at the 4 o'clock spot.

- *I have felt my boss inspire a new idea in me.* (Now you are off and running. Your resistance is gone.) 5 o'clock spot.

- *I am certain my boss has felt me inspire a new idea in him.* 6 o'clock spot.

- *I think we all realize that we are all in this together.* 7 o'clock spot.

- *I would not want to be without this job.* 8 o'clock spot.

- *My boss often asks me to lead projects and direct others.* 9 o'clock spot.

- *It is obvious that he has trust in me.* 10 o'clock spot.

- *I am happy to work with him.* 11 o'clock spot.

And then, in the center of the wheel—right over the top of what you had written before, around the edge of it, or all across the page—in bold, confirming letters, write: *I know my boss sees my value.*

You have moved your Vibration to a new place on this topic, and therefore your point of attraction has shifted and your relationship to your Vortex has shifted. That is Deliberate Creation at its best. In this one short process, you have released resistance, improved your relationship with your boss, brought yourself back into alignment with *who-you-really-are*—and you have entered your Vortex. And now that you are inside the Vortex—you are looking at your world through the eyes of Source.

## The *List-of-Positive-Aspects Process*

Now that you have released your resistance about your employer and established a higher, resistance-free Vibration about this topic, it can be of tremendous value for you to keep this resistance-free ball rolling for the purpose of really establishing your new Vibrational base and point of attraction. In other words, let us milk it for a while and get all of the value we can from the momentum you have going.

So now that you are in alignment with your *Inner Being,* make a list of the positive aspects of your employer and your work from the perspective of Source. From inside the Vortex, this is an easy process to do. And the reason we encourage you to do it is because there is great value in being inside the Vortex. And so, the longer you can stay here, the better.

Now, turn your paper over and write, as a heading at the top of the page: The Positive Aspects of My Employer:

- *He cares about his business.*

- *He is deliberate about who he hires.*

- *He often jumps in to help with a project.*

- *He smiles easily.*

- *People like him.*

- *His business is financially sound.*

- *He got the ball rolling before he hired any of us.*

- *He always makes payroll, and on time.*

- *His business steadily grows.*

- *I'm glad that I work here.*

- *I like what I do.*

- *I really like this man.*

This list may go on even longer, because in your alignment, you are very clear-minded. And so, you will feel the words flowing easily onto your page. You may later be surprised by your flowing compliments of someone who is often annoying, but remember: *in this moment, you are seeing your employer through the eyes of Source.*

## The *Rampage-of-Appreciation Process*

Now if you are really wanting to firmly stake your claim on your newly acquired higher Vibration about this topic, move on to this final process: the *Rampage of Appreciation*. Move to another, clean sheet of paper and begin writing and/or speaking your appreciation for your employer:

*I appreciate . . .*

*. . . his beautiful car.*
*. . . that he puts money back into his business.*
*. . . that he often buys our lunch.*
*. . . our beautiful work space.*
*. . . the scope of this business.*
*. . . where it is going.*
*. . . the potential we all have in working here.*
*. . . the contribution this business offers to the world.*
*. . . the flexibility I have here.*
*. . . his eagerness to learn.*
*. . . how he loves good ideas.*
*. . . his wonderful laugh.*
*. . . his dedication to his business.*
*. . . the stability of his business.*
*. . . the work he offers me.*
*. . . the thrill of adventure.*
*. . . the opportunity to expand.*
*. . . the contrast that helps me expand.*
*. . . my <u>Guidance System</u> that helps me keep up with my expansion.*
*. . . this world.*
*. . . this wonderful time of technology.*
*. . . my life!*

## What Life Is Like, from Inside the Vortex

This book is offered to you to assist you in accepting the existence of your Vibrational Reality Vortex and to inspire within you a desire to go there often, because we have the benefit of existing inside this Vortex that you are creating. From inside your Vortex, we focus upon all that you have asked for and therefore upon that which you have become. As you pay attention to your emotions, and reach steadily for the best-feeling thoughts you can find, you will move into your Vortex whenever you desire; and the more often you are there, the more often you will want to return—because life from inside the Vortex is sublime.

Your point of attraction will be such that only things that are wanted will flow into your path. The people you encounter will be perfect matches to your highest interests, and you will not rendezvous with those not up to speed with who you are. You will feel vital and alive and clear-minded and sure.

You will find the best in others, whether they see it or not. And your appreciation for life will ripple through your body in the form of thrilling sensations as you focus upon the objects of specific appreciation.

But occasionally, even often, you will remember or observe something not up to speed—and your Vortex will spit you out. But do not be alarmed, for you have deliberately emerged into an environment of contrast for the value of the new idea that is always born from the contrast. It is normal to have those *Step One* (asking) moments where you know, so very well, exactly what it is that you do not want. Just remember that, in those moments, you are launching specific rockets of desire into your Vibrational Escrow; and that later, after you have worked the bugs out of your resistance, you can find your way easily back into your Vortex, where you will again reap the benefit of your earlier contrasting moment.

Now that you understand the whole picture, you will find confidence and ease in the Three-Step Process of Creation. When something occurs that causes you to ask (since you now understand the Vortex, and how to get in), you will no longer writhe in the discomfort of powerlessness. No matter what unpleasant problems you may encounter along your way, an improved desire or request will emanate from you, and its solution will amass as all cooperative components assemble, waiting for you to enter the Vortex.

*You do not have to explain this to anyone else; and, in fact, even if you try, they may not understand your words. But it is our promise to you that, through the reading of this book, you now do understand your relationship with the Vortex—and through the power of the example of your joyous life experience, others may be inspired to want to know, also.*

We have enjoyed this interaction immensely.

There is great love here for you, and we remain joyously incomplete.

## — Abraham

# PART VI

# Transcript of Abraham Live: A *Law of Attraction* Workshop

# Transcript of Abraham Live:
# A *Law of Attraction* Workshop

(These *Law of Attraction* workshops were recorded in Asheville, North Carolina, on Sunday, October 19, 2008, and in Chicago, Illinois, on Saturday, September 13, 2008; and this composite session is included on a CD in this book for your listening pleasure. [It has been edited slightly for readability in these pages.] For additional tapes, CDs, books, videos, catalogs, and DVDs, or to reserve your space at an Abraham-Hicks *Law of Attraction* Workshop, please call [830] 755-2299, or write to Abraham-Hicks Publications at P.O. Box 690070, San Antonio, Texas 78269. Also, for an immediate overview of our works, visit our interactive Website at: **www.abraham-hicks.com**.)

### Were You, as an Infant, Trained Negatively?

**Abraham:** Good morning. We are extremely pleased that you are here. It is good to come together for the purpose of co-creating, do you agree? You are knowing what you are wanting? Are you enjoying the expansion of your desire? That's good. This is co-creating at its best, yes?

You know you are more than you see here in these physical bodies? Do you know that you, in your physical body, are extensions of Broader Source Energy? Do you realize that that Broader Non-Physical part of you, that Source within you, is always flowing to you and through you, that you cannot separate yourself from it? Do you realize that that Broader Non-Physical part of you plays a larger role in what happens all day, every day, than most of you know? *The continuum of that which is you is profound—you are Source Energy in a physical body.*

Many of you don't realize that. Often you want to say, "Well, if that's true, then why aren't I doing better? If I'm Source Energy in physical form, then why aren't the angels singing for me more?" And we want you to know that, at all times, the Well-Being that really is you—that surrounds you, that permeates everything in all atmospheres, both physical and Non-Physical—that Well-Being is always flowing to you and through you. And to the degree you *allow* it, you see the evidence of it in your experience.

Often, as you are looking at the details of what's unfolding in your life experience, it feels to you that there must be some outside forces or circumstances—there must be some details—that are keeping you from the Well-Being that we are expressing is yours. Because when the Well-Being isn't flowing—when the money isn't flowing into your experience, or something is hurting in your body, or someone has broken your heart, or something that you want just doesn't seem to come—we know that sometimes it feels to you (because you want it so much to be otherwise), it feels to you that there must be something other than you that is preventing the Well-Being from flowing. But we want you to understand that there is never anything other than you that is preventing the Well-Being from flowing.

Oh, we acknowledge, many times you are born into an environment where Well-Being isn't flowing. Your parents were having a hard time, or the environment into which you were born was in upheaval. And so, as you, even from your infancy, began observing the details of the environment that surrounded you, we acknowledge that it was not hard for you, by virtue of what you were observing, to train your Vibration into one of resistance of the Well-Being that would have been there if you were not trained into resistance.

And many of you say, "There, that's what we're talking about. Why would a wee, small infant be born into an environment where they could, by virtue of the environment that surrounds them, be trained into a resistant Vibration? How could a baby learn a Vibration that prevents Well-Being from flowing?

And we say, because that baby, *that baby that looks like a wee, small, unknowing infant is really a genius Source Energy Deliberate Creator who has come forth into this physical experience not worrying about contrast, and not even wanting to avoid it, but embracing contrast—understanding that from the contrast is always born clarity of improvement.*

And so, often the greatest masters of your physical environment are born into situations where contrast abounds: things they *don't* want all around them, things they *do* want all around them. But let's say you were one (or you know someone) who was born into a very strong environment of contrast. And we want to say to you, as you were born into that strong environment of contrast, the contrast served not only *you*, not only providing expansion for you (which you can beneficially live while still here in this physical body), but that contrast is serving *Mass Consciousness*, and it is certainly serving the *All-That-Is-ness* that is really *you* and all of *us*.

## Your Universe Is Managed by the *Law of Attraction*

So, this Source Energy You remains Non-Physically focused, and a part of you comes forth into this physical body, and the contrast helps you to know what you *don't* want, which causes you to know what you *do* want. Sometimes you really know what you *don't* want, so you really know what you *do* want. Sometimes you sorta know what you *don't* want, so you sorta know what you *do* want. But the contrast is always causing a focusing of Vibration.

Now, whether you speak out loud, whether you even put into words what it is you now know that you want from the contrast that you've lived, you are still emanating the Vibrational signal of it. Many of you say, "Oh, Vibrational signal. Vibrational signal—it doesn't mean anything to me, a Vibrational signal." We say, it means everything to you because you live in a Vibrational Universe that is managed by the *Law of Attraction*, the *Law of Attraction* responding to the Vibrations that abound and managing them—and sorting them—and bringing Vibrations that are alike together. And so, it is important for you to acknowledge that you are Vibrational Beings, constantly emanating Vibrational signals of desire. And here is something really important that you may have forgotten: *When, from your human form, you offer a Vibration of what you want—because you know what you don't want, so you know what you do want—you cannot contemplate any subject without equal components of wanted and unwanted appearing Vibrationally in your experience.*

If you don't have enough money, to the degree that you don't have enough money, you ask for the equal proportion of money to the degree of the money you don't have. (Do you get that?) If you're a *little* sick, you ask to be a *little* well. If you're *a lot* sick, you ask to be *a lot* well. In other words, if you are focused in your physical experience, the proportion of what you *don't* want is represented by a Vibrational equivalent of what you *do* want. (Can you sorta, kinda get that?)

Whether you speak it or not, it is emanating from you. And when that happens, the Non-Physical Source Energy part of you gives undivided attention to that newly added, amended version of the request or desire that you have set forth; and you, from your Non-Physical vantage point, have expanded to that new place—just now.

Now when that happens, that means that the Vibration of the larger part of you (and oh, it is the larger part of you, the Eternal Non-Physical part of you) . . . the Vibration of the larger part of you has changed—ah, so good—because of the contrast you just lived. And if you, who just lived the contrast, could join the larger part of you in the Vibration of what you've asked for, you would have an exhilarating moment, *now.* But you often don't do that.

Often, instead of knowing what you *don't* want, which causes you to know what you *do* want, instead of turning your attention to what you *do* want, you continue to beat the drum of what you *don't* want. And that's not a bad thing, really; it's just, if you keep it up, it doesn't serve you. In other words, what just happened is, life caused you to expand and you didn't go. Life caused you to become more, but you're still justifying why you want more, justifying why you deserve more, lamenting the fact that you aren't more, feeling bad about not getting what you want, complaining about who *is* getting it while you're *not,* adding emphasis to how bad it is over *here* without what it is you want, complaining about being over *here,* explaining how long you've been over *here,* noticing how many other people are over *here,* forming clubs about being over *here* . . . when you want to be over there. [Fun]

Online chat groups: "We're over here, we're over here, we're over here, we're over here, we're over here. And those guys over there, surely they did something wrong. [Fun] They must be cheating. They must be dealing drugs. They must have been born into it. Certainly, they don't deserve it any more than me; and I'm not getting it, I'm not getting it, I'm not getting it. Where's my stuff? Where's my stuff? Where's my stuff? Where's my stuff?" [Fun]

So, you stand (not meaning to) in the Vibration that caused you to do the *asking,* but now you're not asking from the Vibration of *having*—you're asking from the Vibration of *not having.* You see, now, that's normal, isn't it? When you don't have something that you want, from that place of not having it, you're going to ask for it. But can you feel, when you are wadded up in that Vibration of "I don't have something I need; I don't have something I need; I don't have something I need. I want it, where is it? I want it, where is it?"—can you feel how that Vibration is opposite of the Vibration of "I have something that I want"?

The Source within you, in the moment that you ask (oh, this is the part we so want you to hear, because this is the part that explains every emotion you ever feel, or every emotion that anybody ever feels) . . . when the Source within you joins the Vibration of your request and *you* don't—you feel the discord.

Now, let's explain this in a way you can really hear it: If you're not asking for anything beyond what you have—so you're not sending the Source within you to new Vibrational places on your behalf—then you could stand where you are and not feel any discord. The tricky thing about that is, the entire Universe is set up to cause you to expand. *You can't stand still. In every moment, no matter where you stand, there is contrast that is causing you to expand; and if you don't go with the expansion, then you feel the resistance of being pulled apart.*

### Is Your Friend Harassing You into Expansion?

So, when you feel *elation,* it means you expanded; and, in this moment of thought, you went with the expansion. When you feel *love,* it means you've expanded; and, in this moment of thought, you have gone with the thought of *love.* When you feel *interest;* when you feel *excited;* when you feel *passion;* when you're tuned in, tapped in, turned on, that means you expanded . . . and, in this moment, you're not doing that thing you often do that is keeping you from going and being with *who-you-really-are.*

But if, in any moment, you feel *frustration* or *anger* or *fear,* if you feel *powerless,* if you feel those negative emotions that feel so awful to you, all that it means is that, in this moment, you've got something going on in your mind. You're probably talking about it; you're probably blogging about it—you've got something going on in your mind where you are not anywhere near the vicinity of *who-you-really-are.* And the negative emotion that you feel is your *indication* of separation. Now, *separation* is too strong a word, but we want to get your attention with it. *When you feel negative emotion, it simply means you're not keeping up with You.*

Now, there are some important things to know about that: You see, if life wasn't causing you to expand, there would be nothing to keep up with. And you say, "Yes, exactly my point. If contrast were not abounding, then I wouldn't expand. And if I didn't expand, then I wouldn't have to go. I could just sit on my stump." And we say, *no chance,* because you cannot cease to be standing in the middle of a buffet of choices that is causing you to constantly expand.

We are all Eternally focused Beings, which means you are *self-ishly* focused—we *all* are—and we cannot help, at all levels of our Being (even cellular levels), to continue to ask for the improvement, ask for the improvement, ask for the improvement. And, you see, it's sort of tricky, and we see how you might complain. But it goes this way: *If it weren't for the contrast, you couldn't ask for the improvement. But the very contrast that is responsible for the improvement is the contrast that you use as your excuse not to go.* (Isn't that interesting?)

It's like you've got a friend (we use that word loosely) . . . you have a friend who is harassing you into expansion. This friend has been giving you grief for a long time, and you can't shake loose of this friend because you talk about this friend so much that the *Law of Attraction* just keeps that friend right in your space. And even if you are able to remove yourself from the vicinity of that friend by moving across the world—another one takes that friend's place almost immediately. Because when you have something active in your Vibration, the *Law of Attraction* just brings it on, over and over again.

So you have a friend who is harassing you into expansion. That friend is following the nature of his true *selfish* self, and he is doing everything to make *himself* feel better. So, here's this friend harassing you into expansion, and doing it well, because—sort of like a thorn in your side—this friend has been there for a long time; and boy, oh boy, oh boy, has the larger part of you expanded because of the consternation of this relationship. You have expanded and expanded and expanded. So, we could say accurately this friend, who you are not very happy with, is responsible for a huge part of your Vibrational expansion, and the Source within you has benefited dramatically because of this uncomfortable relationship. *So, this friend is responsible for your expansion, but now, here's the interesting part: you, if you're like most people, are now using this friend and this contrasting experience as your excuse now not to keep up with the expansion that this friend caused you to have.*

That's why you're extra, extra, extra mad at this friend. You're tied together Vibrationally. In other words, this friend is a coconspirator in your expansion, but you're using the details of this relationship as your reason not to expand, and that's why you can't get your mind off this rascal. That's why everything seems to be that person's fault. And haven't you noticed that when you've got that sort of thing going on (and almost everybody does, to some degree), for a while it is that person, and then it's *that* person, and then it's *that* person, and then it's *that* person, and then it . . .

In other words, it seems like there's always something that you're using as your current excuse to not let yourself feel good. It's like, "If I could just wrestle this one last rascal to the ground and kill him, then, in the absence of rascaldom, I would feel good."

And we say: *You can't rid the world of things that bother you. You've got to rid your Vibration of things that bother you. And when you rid your Vibration of things that bother you—no things that bother you can come.*

But, you can't *rid* anything from your Vibration, because there is no exclusion in this attraction-based Universe. In an attraction-based Universe, there's only inclusion, which means when you look at this thing you want and you say *yes* to it, you include it in your Vibration. But when you look at this thing you don't want and you shout *no* at it—you include *it* in your Vibration. *The only way that you can stop attracting something that you don't want is by giving your attention to something that you do want. But you have to take small steps in it.*

We really want to give this to you in a way that you will give yourself a little bit of relief: If you've got something active in your Vibration and you've been focused on it for a while, you can't, all of a sudden, switch to another channel just like you do with your radio station. In other words, you can only move incrementally a little bit up the *Emotional Scale*. If you have trained yourself (and that's really a good way of saying it), if you've *trained* yourself into a frequency of complaint about something . . . and we know, it's legitimate. You're not making this stuff up. You've been observing what's going on. We know, they could have done better. They could have been nicer. They could have been more tuned in, tapped in, turned on. If they had been tuned in, tapped in, turned on, all you would have had to do is look at them and you would have felt better. You know it, because there are *some* lovable people in your life. (Not that many, but there are some lovable people in your life.) Most of them are under two. [Fun] But there are some really lovable people in your life . . . or they have fur on them, or feathers. [Fun] Most of them, most people, are not in control of their Vibration. And so, when you say to someone, "I need you to be always in alignment with *who-you-really-are* so that when I look at you, I am then in alignment with *who-I-am*," you're asking the impossible.

*What you have to do is take control of your own Vibration, and say to everyone, "It's not your job to be in alignment in order for me to feel good. It's my job to look around my environment—past, present, and future—*

*for things that line me up with <u>who-I-really-am.</u>"* In other words, you're looking for love in all the wrong places, friends. And the place that you want to look for it, and find it, is this expanded you, the Source Energy you, the part of you that is love—tune yourself to that Vibration.

## All Cooperative Components Are Being Assembled

So let us say that you're using _____ (whatever) as your excuse to not be a Vibrational Match to *who-you-are*. . . . And you're using your *Guidance System,* that's what your *emotions* are. Your emotions are your *indicator:* The better you feel, the more you've *closed* the gap between you and You. . . . The worse you feel, the more you've *widened* the gap between you and You. If you are chronically complaining and not feeling good, it means you've trained yourself into a Vibration that just won't let life get really good for you. So you say, "Well, I've got a lot to complain about."

And we say, we imagine you do, because when you've trained yourself into a complaining Vibration, the Well-Being is hindered by your habit of thought.

So then you say, "Well, how do I untrain myself?"

And we say, by reaching, as often as you can—consciously and deliberately—for the best thought about the active subject that you can find from where you are. By reaching for the *best* of it rather than the *worst* of it. By beating the drum of the *Wouldn't it be nice if . . . ?*'s instead of beating the drum of *Wouldn't it be awful if . . . ?* By beating the drum of *I really like this about that* instead of the drum of *What I really don't like about that is . . .*

If we can somehow convince you that you are a Source Energy Vibration that is powerfully calling you to the Well-Being that you deserve, and if you will listen to the call of that Source and Vibrationally feel for it, and listen and move consistently in the direction of the thoughts that feel better, you will, before you know it, close the Vibrational gap between *you* and *You* on every subject that's active within you; and you will then be the joyous, progressive, fulfilled, intuitive, loving, vital, exhilarated Being that you were born to be. It isn't a hard thing once you understand the way it all works. In other words, if you take away from this gathering only the understanding that you are Source Energy and that when you are here in this physical body, if you're not letting yourself vibrate in alignment with *who-you-really-are,* you're just not going to feel good.


## Getting into Your Powerful Vortex of Attraction

Here is the way the Creative Process works: So you were Source Energy. Part of you came forth into this body. You're mixing it up with others; and you are sending constant rockets of desire forward, forward, where the Source within you is taking them.

Now, do you understand that everything that exists around you is an extension, or an expanded version, of a previous Vibration? Everything is *Vibration* first, before it becomes *thought-form,* or before it takes form. So, even this world that you see spinning in its orbit was, at one time, only a concept, a Vibrational concept. And here you are now, full-fledged human Beings, with all of your physical beingness, interpreting, Vibrationally, this time-space reality. . . . *Everything that you know around you as the real physical stuff—is just an extension of thought.*

Everything that is coming in your future is now already fulfilled, Vibrationally, in what we are calling your *Vibrational Reality.* (We have been calling it your Vibrational Escrow.)

Now, there are a lot of people scoffing, "Oh, Vibrational Reality." *We say, you must not scoff at Vibrational Reality because all "reality" came from Vibrational Reality. And it comes fast if you will allow it.*

You are on the Leading Edge. The manifestation time between the inception of thought and the lining up with it is seconds in many cases. You are on the brink of instant manifestation, in many cases, for this reason: You are not new to creation, you are longtime creators, and you have set a lot into motion even before you came into this physical body. You had a Vibrational Escrow brewing before your feet even hit the ground here. And now, with the last conversation you had with someone, with the last thing you watched on television, with the last book you read, with the last movie you went to, with the last thought you thought, you have been contributing to this Vibrational Escrow; and it is brewing. No, it is *swirling*. It is a gigantic *Vortex of Attraction*. (Now, you've been hearing about the *Law of Attraction*, but few are even coming close to understanding the power of the *Law of Attraction*. This is the *Law* that creates worlds.) So, here is this swirling Energy. How'd it get there? You put some of it there before you were even born. You've been putting it there every day of your physical experience. . . .

So, here is this *Vortex of becoming*. This *Vortex of becoming.* This Vibration—this pure Vibration of all the things that you want, all the amended details that you've been asking for—here it is swirling, swirling, swirling, swirling. And the *Law of Attraction is summoning all* (hear this), *all cooperative parts to it.*

What do we mean? *Cooperative parts,* meaning "things of a Vibrational Match." So, you didn't have a lover; you *asked* for a lover. You had a lover with no money; you *asked* for a lover with more money. You had a lover who didn't like you very much; you *asked* for a lover who really likes you. You had a lover who didn't share your values; you *asked* for a lover who shared your values.

In other words, you've been building this Escrow, and this Escrow is Vibrationally vivid and real and attracting. So, *here* is your request on all kinds of subjects. And *there,* as your request is pulsing, because it's being tended . . . no, it's being known—no, it's being *be'd*—by the Source within you, the *Law of Attraction, the powerful Law that creates worlds, is amassing all cooperative places, people, events, things: all things necessary to fulfill what you've been asking for are being drawn by this powerful Vortex of Attraction.*

The question we want to put to you is: Are you cooperating? Are you cooperating with your own desire?

"No, I'm bummed that I don't have it."

Are you a Vibrational Match to your lover?

"No, I'm mad at the one I've got."

Are you a Vibrational Match to the Well-Being that you're asking for?

"No, no, I've joined an online chat group, and we complain. [Fun] We complain all day about how bad it is. . . . No, I am, in my human form, the one uncooperative component of my creation."

So, what happens to your creation? Do others get it? No, they've got their own going.

"So, will my creation go away?"

No, it'll just get bigger.


### *Contrast* Really Isn't about Something Going Wrong

*We want you to reach the place where you are* <u>*willing*</u> *. . . not just willing,* <u>*determined*</u> *. . . not just determined,* <u>*eager*</u> *. . . to let go of the need of control of things that are uncontrollable—like what anybody else is doing—and give your undivided attention to the only thing you* <u>*can*</u> *control, which is how you* <u>*feel*</u> *in any given circumstance.* In other words, we want you to leave this gathering saying, "I've decided that I'm going to take life as it comes, and I'm going to do the best that I can do in the midst of what I'm doing."

Nothing ever goes wrong, because every piece of contrast, no matter how wrong it seems to be, is always helping you to clarify what it is you *do* want. And that's the thing that we want you to remember most of all: *The contrast, no matter how it looks in any moment, is contributing mightily to your expansion. And the things that you call "things going wrong" in your life experience are actually only the distance between the things that are so right and your current perspective about it.* In other words, if you could just accept that you have amassed a huge Vibrational fortune that is ready for you to begin tapping into immediately, and all that is required in order to tap into it is a willingness to look in the direction of what you want—which will cause you to no longer look in the direction of what you don't want—life will begin to get better for you, right now.

And that is our strongest message to you: *Life is supposed to be good for you.* You live, whether you know it or not . . . you live as the full recipients of a hurricane of grace that is flowing toward you, at all times, in answer to all that you have been asking for. Not one of you has been separated out as one who should not be the receiver of it. All of you are in the full flow of this hurricane of Well-Being. And as you understand that, and you begin to stand up with an attitude of willingness to receive the benefit of this Well-Being and worthiness that's flowing to you at all times, as you just get a whiff of that . . . and the best way to get a whiff of it is to stand right where you are, right now, and do your best to find the best of the positive aspects that surround you. Look for things to appreciate, even if there aren't that many. Look for things to feel good about, even if there are more things to feel bad about. Give your attention, as best you can, to the best things that are going on in your experience, with the determination to train yourself into the best-feeling Vibration that you can find right here and now.

*Today, no matter where I'm going, no matter what I'm doing, no matter who I'm doing it with, it is my dominant intent to look for and find things that feel good when I see them, when I hear them, when I smell them, when I taste them, when I touch them. It is my dominant intent to solicit, experience, and exaggerate and talk about and revel in, the best of what I see around me here and now.* As that is your mantra, you will tune yourself to the best Vibration that you can reach for, and then the best, and then the best, and then the best—and then the best. And then, before you know it, you will be vibrating in the vicinity of what's going on in your Vibrational Escrow, in your Vibrational Reality.

### Are You Ready to Meet Your Vortex?

This Vibrational Reality is spinning and becoming, and if you are in *anger* or *fear* or *despair,* you're nowhere near it. When you get in the vicinity of *hope,* when you start feeling hopeful, you're within range. When you feel hopeful, it's drawing you in; it's drawing you in. And once you begin to *believe* or *expect* good things to come—you're in the Vortex. And once you get in there, you're no longer the only uncooperative component. Now you are a cooperative component. Now you get to rendezvous with your money. You get to rendezvous with your vitality. You get to rendezvous with your clarity. You get to rendezvous with your lover, with your loving neighbor, with the things of your environment that you've been wishing for. *You get to rendezvous with all of the good stuff that you've put there once you begin to get in the vicinity of what feels good. And you can <u>train</u> yourself there—you can do it in a day.*

By tomorrow, you could be Vibrationally so close to *who-you-are* that you would begin to see the evidence. You would begin to see movement: your bank account will shift toward what you are wanting; the people in your neighborhood will begin to be more cooperative. . . . *You have control of everything that rendezvous with you when you get control of the Vibration that you offer, and you get control of the Vibration that you offer when you care about how you feel.*

When you care about how you feel and you lean in the direction of what feels best, you become, in a very short time, a Vibrational Match to *who-you-have-become.* And then people who are watching you say, "What happened to you? You're just happy all the time, and every time I turn around, some other wonderful thing is coming to you."

And you say, "I got in the Vortex."

And they say, "What?"

You say, "Yeah, I got into the Vortex, and I'm in the Vortex."

"What? How do you get in? Where's the door? Where's the door? I want in, too."

And you say, "Well, you've got your own, and you have to *feel* your way in. There's not a written script. There's not a detailed manual. There's not an obvious door. There's not a combination lock. *You just feel your way in.*"

"Well, how do you know if you're on the track?"

"You *feel* better than you just did."

"Well, I feel like *revenge.*"

"Well, you're probably moving in the right direction. Because right before *revenge,* how did you feel?"

"Well, before *revenge* I felt *powerless.* Now I'm feeling *revenge.*"

"Good. You're on the path."

"I'm feeling *revenge* and I'm on the path to the Vortex of Well-Being?"

"Yeah, yeah. Just don't go back to *powerlessness*, and you'll be on the path."

"What comes after *revenge?*"

"*Anger.* You'll be real mad at a lot of people."

"Oh, I've been there."

"Well, go there again, because when you're *angry,* you're on the path. *Anger* is better than *revenge.* It's closer to your Vortex."

"What comes after that?"

"*Frustration. Overwhelment. Pettiness.*"

"Hmm, hmm, I can sort of get that. What comes after that?"

"*Hope.*"

"Haven't had any of that in a long time."

"Well, then, look forward to it. Look forward to *hope* because when you get (you can say to your friend) in the vicinity of *hope,* you'll get in the Vortex. Occasionally (every day) something will happen that will give you evidence that you are the Deliberate Creator of your experience. If you can hang around in *hope,* even only on two or three subjects, you'll get in the Vortex enough that you will come to *believe.* If you can make your way to *hope*—and it's not hard—you'll get in the Vortex often enough that you'll start to *believe.*"

"Believe what?" your friend will say.

- *You'll begin to believe in the power of your thought.*

- *You'll begin to believe in the goodness of this Universe.*

- *You'll begin to believe in the worthiness of your Being.*

- *You'll begin to believe in the power of <u>who-you-are.</u>*

- *You'll begin to believe in the cooperative <u>Law of Attraction.</u>*

- *You'll begin to believe that all things are possible.*

- *You'll begin to believe that you are the creator of your own reality.*

- *You'll begin to believe that you can control your thoughts by paying attention to the way you feel.*

- *You will begin to believe that you can be or do or have anything.*

"That's what I know," you will tell your friend, "now that I am in the Vortex."

And what is the *Vortex?* It's just the Vibrational, advanced announcement of who you have become. All the cooperative parts of the Universe have already been gathered there. They are there, waiting for you. Don't you just love knowing that? Waiting for you. Waiting for you.

So, what's the holdup? "I don't like this, and I don't like this, and I don't like this, and I don't like this." Really insignificant, unimportant, petty little things that you're using, from your day-to-day experience—that you're using as your excuse not to get in the Vortex. Isn't that lazy? When you could just as easily look for a *hopeful* thought as a *pessimistic* thought. You could just as easily look for a *compliment* as something *derogatory.* You could just as easily *praise* your government . . . no, let's start with something easier. [Fun] You could just as easily look for a reason to feel good as a reason to feel bad. You could just as easily turn your television off as turn it on.

## The *Law of Attraction* and *Law*-Based Premises

So, as we come together, whether you are reading something we have written or listening to anything that we have ever said, we want you to understand that everything we offer, and every word Esther translates from our Vibration, is offered with the intention of helping you to restore your awareness of the valid premises that match the *Laws of the Universe.* Because when you start consciously understanding the *Laws* as they are, and you test them from that conscious awareness of them, they will prove to you, every single time, without exception, the validity of these truths:

- You are the creator of your own reality.

- You were worthy before you focused into this physical body, and you still are now that you've been here, no matter what.

- You are more Non-Physical Source Energy Vibration than you are the flesh, blood, and bone Being that you see here in these physical bodies.

- The *Law of Attraction* is responding to everyone equally across the board.

- The *Law of Attraction*, which responds to everything and everyone, says, *That which is like unto itself, is drawn,* so whatever Vibration is active, the *Law of Attraction* is making it more active by bringing more things that match it to it.

- You are Source Energy, with a perspective that the *Law of Attraction* is responding to; and you are physically focused, Leading Edge, genius creators, out here on the Leading Edge of thought in your magnificent bodies in this time-space reality of perfect diversity—and the *Law of Attraction* is responding to that aspect of you, too.

- As the *Law of Attraction* responds to both Vibrational aspects of you, you feel the harmony, or not, of those two Vibrational relationships. The better you feel, the more *that* physical part of you is in sync with *this* part of you. The worse you feel, the more that part of you, *that* physical part of you, is out of sync with *this* part of you.

- When life, in your physical form, causes you to know what you *don't* want, it causes you to know—whether you speak it or not—what you *do* want. And when that occurs, you emanate a Vibrational request that the larger part of you receives and responds to and becomes immediately—and the *Law of Attraction,* in that instant, begins responding to that newly formed Vibrational version of you.

- There is a *Vibrational Reality* that is amassing constantly, which is the true you. There is the *physical* reality, the knock-on-wood, manifested, actualized, "I can see it, taste it, smell it, hear it, touch it" reality; and that reality is only slightly different than the *Vibrational Reality* in that what's already manifested . . . you've just been thinking about it long enough that now it's showing up to give you awareness of how you've been vibrating.

- Everything that you are living is a manifestational indicator of your mix of Vibrations.

- The Well-Being that is you, that is in constant process of becoming, is so huge and so long lasting (in that it is Eternal) that Well-Being will always triumph—but some have to croak to experience it.

These *Law of Attraction* seminars, where we emphasize understanding the *Art of Allowing* (which is finding Vibrational alignment with *who-I-really-am*), we offer them to assist you in coming into Vibrational alignment with *who-you-really-are;* to live life as you intended; and to be the uplifted, good-feeling, Pure, Positive Energy radiator, oozer, *be*-er of the love that is truly you.

*The most dominant premise that is misunderstood in your physical reality is that when someone performs something that you disapprove of, it is a good idea for you to point it out, or you might get more of it.* When the reality of it is, the more you point at what you *do not* want, the more you hold yourself in a consistent pattern of Vibration that disallows what you *do* want.

The most powerful premise that we want to activate within you, that, we promise you, will serve you for all of the days of your life is: *A belief is only a thought I keep thinking. A belief is only a thought I continue to think. A belief is only my habit of thought; it's only a practiced thought—a belief is only a thought that I think a lot.*

Now why does that matter? Because when you want something and you *believe* in opposition to it, your opposite *belief* will prevent what you want from happening. When you want something and you *believe* it, there's no separation; you are offering one signal, and the *Law of Attraction* will bring it to you *now*. But when you want something and you *doubt* it—when you want it and you *don't believe* it—now you're offering opposing Vibrations, and you can hold yourself in that holding pattern all of the days of your life.

"I want it but . . ."; "I want it but . . ."; "It'd be nice, but it doesn't happen for me"; "I would really like to have that, but I've wanted it for so long. . . ." When you keep saying those things, when you continue to *face reality,* when you beat the drum of *what-is,* when you beat the drum of *what-is*—you hold active within yourself a Vibrational pattern. (A belief is only a thought you keep thinking.)

*A belief is only a thought that you keep thinking—and it is only the beliefs that you hold that keep you from the things that you want. A belief is only a thought that you keep thinking. And the only thing that keeps you from <u>who-you-really-are</u> and what you really want is a belief, which is only a thought that you keep thinking.* (Did you write that down?) [Fun]

"So, if a belief is only a thought that I keep thinking, and I keep thinking a thought that is in opposition to what I want—*then the reason I don't get what I want is because I keep thinking a thought that's in opposition to what I want.*"

Isn't this interesting? Obvious, but interesting, in a whole new sort of decisive way. "So, if a belief is only a thought that I keep thinking, what about thinking a thought that I don't believe long enough that I believe it? If a belief's only a thought that I keep thinking, why not think a *hopeful* thought?"

"That's stupid, Abraham. The facts defy it. The facts . . ."

Oh well, that's that false premise that we were talking about, isn't it? That really is static.

"So, you mean I have been building my life on a false premise by facing reality and feeling that that legitimized giving my attention to this unwanted thing?"

Even Esther will say, occasionally, "But Abraham, but it's true, but it's true," as if that is any prerequisite for what you give your attention to.

A belief is only a thought that you keep thinking. And you, as human Beings, are the harborers of so many unproductive beliefs, the largest among them: *I'm not worthy. . . . There's no gain without pain. . . . I must have been born under the wrong star. . . . Must be karma. . . . Probably my mother's fault. . . . It's the government's fault. . . .* [Fun] You want to believe *that* false premise, don't you? *It's the government's fault. If they'd be different, everything would be different.*

We want to say to you, take your power back by remembering that a belief is only a thought that you keep thinking. "A belief is only a thought that I keep thinking. A belief is only a thought that I keep thinking. A belief is only a thought that I keep thinking. I'm starting to believe that. [Fun] A belief is only a thought that I keep thinking. A belief is only a thought that I keep thinking. When I think a thought, it activates a Vibration; and when a Vibration is activated, my point of attraction kicks in. So if I keep thinking this same thought, and I keep activating this point of attraction, and *Law of Attraction* keeps responding to this active Vibration, then *I'm going to continue to get results, not because they're <u>true,</u> and not because it's <u>reality,</u> but because it's the <u>Law of Attraction</u>'s consistent response to a thought that I keep thinking.*"

So if it's a thought that you keep thinking, and you're getting results that you *don't* want, wouldn't it be prudent to begin to think a different thought?

"Oh, but Abraham, that doesn't seem logical. You want me to think an airy-fairy pretend thought? You want me to put my head in the clouds, or in the sand? You want me to pretend that something that isn't, *is?*"

*Yes.*

"You want me to fantasize? You want me to imagine? You want me to use words that aren't true?"

*Yes.*

"You want me to pretend that I'm slender when I'm fat?"

*Yes.*

"You want me to pretend that I'm prosperous when I'm poor?"

*Yes.*

*We want you to think the thoughts that match what you want until you believe them. And when you think the thoughts that match what you want until you believe them, Universal Forces will give you the proof of your belief. But if you need to see it before you believe it, it cannot come. You have to believe it before you see it.*

What's a *belief*?

"A belief is just a thought I keep thinking."

So what did we just say? You have to keep thinking the thought until it becomes; you have to keep thinking the thought until you believe it—and when you believe it—it is. It's so simple. (We are done.) [Fun] So what distracts you from that? *Reality. Facts.* So what? *Everything that you see that you call reality is just coagulated, coalesced, combined thought—a thought that somebody thought long enough.*

When Esther asks, "Abraham, shouldn't I think about that because it's true?" we say, all *truth* is, is something that enough people, or a person, gave enough attention to long enough that it became a thought that they thought about and thought about and thought about and thought about and thought about it—until it attracted its equivalent.

There are all kinds of things in your environment—that you believe—that match what you want. And there are all kinds of things in your environment that you believe that defy what you want. How would you ever sort them out? *How do you know the active beliefs within you that serve you well and the active beliefs that are within you that don't serve you? How do you know the beneficial ones from the detrimental ones? The beneficial beliefs feel better when you think them. The detrimental ones feel worse when you think them.*

"Oh, but Abraham, there are a lot of thoughts I think that I don't really have much feeling around."

Keep thinking them; they'll get bigger and pretty soon, you'll know. In other words, that's the beauty of the *Law of Attraction:* In the early, subtle stages, you might not be able to feel the difference. But the longer you think them, the more active they become; the more active they become, the more attraction power; the more attraction power, the more obvious the results. Just like you knew it would be. . . . This is the perfect environment for a creator to create, and you knew it when you came.

So, what do you want to talk about? We're eager to talk with you about anything that's important. Nothing is off-limits. It will be a perfect unfolding. Don't worry if you don't get called to the chair, because someone *will* be called who will address what you want to talk about.

This gathering gathered before you dragged your physical bodies here, so there is nothing that you want to talk about that we will not address completely. There *is* some small issue about whether you'll *hear* it or not, but we promise that we will talk about it completely. And, depending upon your vicinity to the Vortex that has already been created and this masterful unfolding of Leading Edge thought, while you'll hear it, or you won't, we'll do our best to draw you in so that you *can* hear it completely. Hmm . . . we're going to have a very good day. Begin right there.

### Must a Child *Earn* Its Well-Being?

**Questioner:** We have a child. He's six years old now. He's been with us two years, and we call him the Abraham child—he came to be through creation (through *allowing*), and he's pretty joyous and pretty special. I'm at a point now where we believe that he can have what he wants and what he desires, but when he asks *me* for things, I don't like that. "Can I have a toy? Can I have that candy bar? Can I have this? Can I have that?" There's a struggle within me, of saying, "Yes, here's the money. Go get what you want. You can have what you want." I mean, it's not harmful what he's asking for; it's just that I'm trying not to . . . I don't know *what* I'm trying to do. . . . But it's very difficult to just openly give. And yet, in my Abraham teachings, I think he should be able to have what he wants. If we have the means to give to him anything he wants, and it's not harmful, I'm torn between *Why can't he have it?* but then I go, *Well, wait a minute now—can you just openly give like that to a child?*

**Abraham:** Well, it sounds like we're on the brink of uncovering another flawed premise: *Spare the rod, spoil the child.* (Yeah, yeah, you been beating him up a lot lately?) [Fun]

**Questioner:** If you asked him, he'd say yes.

**Abraham:** We realize that this is a premise that you got from us. In other words, you've heard us say, on endless occasions, that when you do for someone else, it's like saying "I do this for you because I see you cannot do it," and so that's the contradiction that you're feeling within yourself. You want to be an avenue for inspiration, but you don't want to be the *only* Vortex through which his Well-Being flows.

But if he is asking from a place of pure expectation, and you have an impulse of wanting to offer, then you are just a compliant component of the Universe. In other words, you and your means have been drawn into his Vibrational Escrow, and you are one of the cooperative components in helping him to achieve whatever it is that he is wanting.

So, we would say to you, the only thing that you want to be aware of is, if you are giving from your *desire* to give, not from your *responsibility* to give, it can never get out of whack. In other words, if he asks from his place of pure wanting and pure expectation, you can hardly deny it. But if he gets out of whack and is wanting because it will fill a void for him and he is feeling needy, so to you it *feels* off—then it's *off*.

**Questioner:** Or he sometimes asks from a place of thinking I'm not going to give it to him, so he's not aligned in his asking, either.

**Abraham:** Precisely. And you don't want to upset his applecart by showing him a flawed premise. In other words, if he's in this place where he doesn't *expect* you to give it, and you override your Guidance and his Guidance and give up the goods, you are presenting to him a flawed premise, and that's what's bugging you. [**Questioner:** Yeah, it's difficult.] So what you want to constantly say to yourself, to him—to anyone—is: "When you're tuned in, you are undeniable; and I, and all other components of the Universe, have to yield to you. But when you're not tuned in, when you're begging, when you're pleading, when you're needing, when you're asking from a place of not being lined up with it, then it doesn't happen as easily."

Here's what you basically want to convey, whether he's old enough to hear it through your verbal description or not, but this is the premise that you want to convey through the clarity of your example: (this is you:) *It's my intention to be so in tune with my Source that anything that matches that brings us all to that same vicinity—and it unfolds. But I do not want to be someone who tries to compensate for your misalignment. So, your alignment is what I always strive for. Your alignment is your greatest gift to you, your greatest gift to me. My alignment is my greatest gift to me, my greatest gift to you; and that's what I'm wanting to demonstrate.*

And you can do it, in a way that he will come to understand, when you just ask the simple question: <u>*What*</u> *is it that you want, and* <u>*why*</u> *do you want it?* And as he explains that he wants it because he doesn't have it, then you want to playfully laugh and say, "Well, that's a screwy reason. When you want something because you don't have it, then I'm inspired to add to the *not-having-it* part, instead of the *having-it* part. But when you want something because it'll be fun, then I'm inspired to be in on that." In other words, that's what you want to *show* him.

**Questioner:** That's great. Yeah, that's nice.

**Abraham:** And he's already begun to pick that up, but because you're not utterly consistent, he's confused.

**Questioner:** Yeah, you're right. I felt like I was in the way of his creation, so . . .

**Abraham:** Well, you could say to him, "You know, if you'd leave me out of your equation, you could probably create way bigger, because I have. . . ."

**Questioner:** Well, that's what I thought. He could just have it; why am *I* in there?

**Abraham:** Because it's fun.

**Questioner:** Oh.

**Abraham:** Why is he in your life?

**Questioner:** Because it's fun and joyful.

**Abraham:** Because it's fun. . . . In other words, you were all in each other's Vibrational Escrows, and the *Law of Attraction* brought you all together. And the *Law of Attraction's* bringing all that other stuff together, too; and it's fun, you see. But there is a premise that is flawed that goes like, "I don't want to spoil him, and I don't want to give him the feeling that he just has to ask for it and I'll give it to him." And we say, why not?

"Well, I might be there, and in my love for him . . . I might always give it to him. But when he gets out in the real world, he'll be ill-prepared for the real world."

And we say, he won't be ill-prepared for the world that *Law of Attraction* sets up with him if you don't give it to him if he's not in alignment, and if he's not in alignment and if you're not in alignment—you can't give it to him. And so, that's not preparing him falsely for the way *Law of Attraction* will treat him.

*Make a nucleus right there in your home that mimics the* <u>*Law of Attraction,*</u> *as you know it to be, and you will prepare yourself and your child for anything that the world can throw at him, you see. It's the parents who distort the* <u>*Laws of the Universe*</u> *with these false premises that leave their children ill-prepared when they get out into the world.*

*Alignment* is the big factor; and everything else is really not even secondary, but way, way, way, way down the list. And there are so many people who are (that's this false-premise business that we are talking about), who are making decisions about what's right and wrong, and they're disregarding alignment—when alignment is everything.

We know. You're right when you say (because many parents say it) that it is difficult, because you're trying to lay out the ground rules for your children. You want them to thrive, and you don't want them to play in the street, and you don't want them to eat ground glass, and you don't want them to play with perverts in the park. In other words, there are all kinds of things that you feel guarded against. *And we just want to say to you that when you teach* *them alignment through the offering of your own alignment, and you let that be the cornerstone of your relationship with them—now you've given them something that they can <u>always,</u> always count on.*

So the perfect answer, when he asks for something that doesn't feel good to you, is: "You know, I don't know why, but this feels really *off* to me. And there's one thing that I've always promised myself, especially when it regards you. *If it doesn't feel good, I'm not going to do it until I can bring it into alignment.* So, if I can make this sound like a good idea to me, which means I'm in alignment with the whole of me, then we'll proceed. But until then, don't ask me to do something that feels so *off* to me." That's the example that you want to give to your children. *I never take action when I'm out of alignment. I never take action when something feels off. . . . <u>I never take action when something feels off—and it doesn't have anything to do with how much you want it—I never take action when something feels off.</u>*

And oh, wouldn't you just love for your little one, on the playground or anywhere someone is trying to talk him into doing something . . . and he says, *"I never do anything when something feels off."* [**Questioner:** I'd love it.] *"I just don't do things . . ."*

"Come and steal candy in this store with me. I do it all the time, and it's really fun."

*"I never do anything when it feels off."* [**Questioner:** That is great.]

"Oh, come on, come on, we won't get caught. It's all right. It's only breaking a little rule. No one will know."

*"I never do anything when it feels off."*

"Well, why not? You chicken."

"Well, it's feeling even more off now. [Fun] *You* feel off to me. I don't think I want to play with you; you feel off to me. You feel off to me. I don't play with people who feel off, and I don't do things that feel off. I'm addicted to alignment. I learned it from my dad."

Have you ever had anybody say, "I bet you're *not* going to do that," and you think, *You'd better believe I'm <u>not</u> going to do it. I can't buck your current. I can't buck your negative expectation.* Have you ever had anybody try to prod you into something from their place of *not* expecting? Now, we're exaggerating this way out of proportion, but we just want you to realize that you've got to get over there where your dream for this child is . . .

**Questioner:** And stay there, yeah.

**Abraham:** You don't have to *stay* there. You just have to know the *Laws of the Universe* (and you do) and get rid of those flawed premises—and just remember that you can never consistently *motivate* anybody to anything.

Oh, they'll do it if you're bigger and stronger and if you make the consequences big enough. You can even break a horse (and a horse is big), but you never end up with a joyous beast, ever. But when you see the *best* of them, and you go over to where your version of the best of them is, and you align with *that,* and offer one signal—now you are part of the *inspiration,* you see.

*Haven't you ever had that experience yourself when someone sees you and loves you and expects the best of you? Don't you shine in ways you never shined before? And don't you find it really hard to shine when somebody doesn't feel that way about you?*

We want everybody else to be irrelevant to you, and we would say that to everyone. We would like everybody to release the peanut gallery (which includes their parents) and deal with their own Vibrational gap. But you are a Deliberate Creator who wants, more than life itself, to get a handle on this and to pass it on to this child. [**Questioner:** Absolutely.] And what a lucky boy this is, and we mean *lucky* in the sense of the word that you understand it. It has nothing to do with *luck,* but what a fortunate person he is to have come into an environment where his parents are actually trying to learn how to play by the rules of the Universe that are consistent rather than flawed.

**Questioner:** I think you've already given me this, but as I was sitting there, I said, *If I could speak to God* (which, as you said, I am). . . . What are the big three, the 1-2-3 of child raising?

**Abraham:** *He's perfect as he is, and becoming more. . . . He didn't come here to satisfy my intentions. . . . It's my job to work what he does* *around in my mind so that I feel good. . . . It's not his responsibility to please me.* That was four, but . . .

**Questioner:** Thank you.

## Are There Proper Expectations of Lovers?

**Questioner:** Thank you. I appreciate this opportunity for a Vibrational checkup. I need it. I get a lot of your references to relationships and the emphasis on not being dependent upon another to meet your needs. And I get that.

**Abraham:** Because they will let you down every time because it's not their job.

**Questioner:** Right. And I get that, especially early on. First it was vis-à-vis emotional needs, and not looking to somebody to make you whole, that kind of thing, because I had had that perspective through the years. And as part of that commentary on how many of us currently look at the definition of *commitment* and *expectation* to do this and that "until death," or "Jump through these hoops, and I'll be happy." Um . . .

**Abraham:** False premise, false premise, false premise. [Fun]

**Questioner:** And I'm another one who has listened to you too much, so . . .

**Abraham:** And it's not even over yet.

**Questioner:** And you said those things are not only too rigid, they're unrealistic. Makes perfect sense.

**Abraham:** Because they're based on false premises. We really want to drive that one home. *You can't start out with something that's corrupt at its base—and ever make it work, without more creativity than it's worth.*

**Questioner:** Clearly, this is the day of false premises. But it also sounds like, at times, when you're describing this dynamic, you come right up to the edge of saying that . . . that might include *expectations* of monogamy. Or that might include *expectations* of somebody being there for you when times are hard. Or other kinds of *expectations*.

So my question is: *Are there any expectations of another in a relationship that are not unrealistic and too rigid?*

**Abraham:** Well, here's the thing. Of course, it is appropriate for you to sift through your buffet of choices and find your preferences. What's screwy is picking one person and asking them to match your preference rather than put your preferences over there in your Vibrational Reality, letting the *Law of Attraction* bring it all together—and then you reaping the benefit of what you've sown. That's quite different. In other words, you, of course, get to selectively sift. You get to choose, with great definition, the details of what pleases you. And every bit of that is wonderful. Just don't ask that person now to be all those things. That's what gets screwy.

*Let your Vibrational Escrow percolate, and you do your best to give it your undivided attention so that you become a Vibrational Match to it. And then, when the* Law of Attraction *brings all of it together and brings you, because you're a match, together with it—then there aren't any bugs to work out.*

But what you are describing goes more like this: You sift through the data, and you define what you *want,* but you don't work on becoming a match to what you *want.* So, you give your attention to what you've *got.* In giving your attention to what you *got,* you're not a Vibrational Match to what you *want.* And now you say, "I'm not disciplined enough to look at what I *want;* I'm looking at what I've *got.* So I guess *you* need to change to meet all my *expectations.* If you'd be like that, then I'd be whole." That's what goes screwy.

*Don't ask the person, or people, that helped you to __define__ what you want to __become__ what you want so that you can __have__ what you want. (Oh, that was so good.) Instead, let them be the __Step One__ part of it (the asking part). Use your willpower and your decision to focus upon what you want—and then the Universe will bring you what you want.*

There are so many people who are going about it from a flawed-premise, backwards way, where they say, "I'd feel better if you'd act more like *that*, and I resent that you don't love me enough to try."

And if the others could speak it like it really is, they'd say, "Hey, it's not my job to be everything that you want. It was my job to harass you into clarity about what you want. And now that you're clear about what you want, can't you see *I'm* not it? Don't try to make me be it. Focus upon what you want and let *that* come to you, and leave me alone!"

"No, I want *you* to be it. You inspired my desire, and if you hadn't made me grow, I wouldn't be having this problem. So, you owe it to me to be what I grew to." [Fun]

*Here's something really worth remembering: When you stand where you are, knowing that you want something that hasn't come about yet, and you don't have the discipline to look in the direction of what you want, but instead, you're looking at whatever it was that caused you to want it and you're feeling the discord of that lack of focus—there is a very powerful tendency, without even knowing it, to let what you've got be the catalyst that trains your Vibration. So, you keep thinking <u>this</u> thought, which is different from what you want, but you keep thinking the thought. So, you develop a belief and/or a chronic pattern of thought, which then holds you apart from what you want.*

So, the best way we have of describing that is, let's say that you are interacting with someone who causes you to want *this*. And if you could give *this* that you want your undivided attention, then you would stand there and the Universe would have to deliver to you that. So, it is really a common thing that someone who wasn't giving it to you now gives it to you because you've lined up your Vibration, and so anything less than that is illogical.

And you threw in some words like *monogamy*. If you were someone who wants that, and you are interacting with someone who doesn't, or other way around (it doesn't make any difference . . . you want it and they don't), and you focus upon *what you want* and *why you want it*—the Universe has to bring you what you want. But if you focus upon what the *other* wants, which you *don't want*, then, without meaning to, you train your Vibration to what you *don't want,* and then you can't get what *you* want. And you keep thinking it's the other person's fault, when the only thing that ever comes to you is what's active in your Vibration.

This is just another way of saying to you, you've got to let everybody else off the hook, and you've just got to develop your own deliberate pattern of thought by focusing upon what you want. *Stop asking other people to be big players in giving you what you want, and you be the only player in becoming a match to what you want—and then watch how fast the Universe delivers to you exactly what you want. And when that happens, then you're able to live and let live. Then you're able to let the world be whatever it individually chooses to be, because it can't hinder you or keep you from what you want. It never could, but sometimes it feels like it could.*

It's like the Tabasco-sauce-in-the-pie story that we used to tell. "There's Tabasco sauce in this kitchen; I know it's going to get in my pie."

It's not going to get in your pie.

"Well, it's in the kitchen; it might get in my pie."

It's not going to get in your pie.

"Well, it's in the kitchen and it might get in my pie, and I'd feel a lot better if it wasn't in the kitchen. [Fun] Get it out of the kitchen so it can't get in my pie. Oh look, it's in my pie! I told you. I told you. I told you it'd get in my pie because it's in the kitchen."

And we say, *it didn't get in your pie because it's in the kitchen. It got in your pie because you couldn't get your eyes off of it. It got in your pie because you kept talking about it, kept activating the Vibration of it.*

It really is more irrelevant than you think what the other people in your life want, but what *is* relevant is what you think they want. So, if you could just eternally look toward what *you* want and disregard everything else, the Universe would have to give you what you want, and in so many more cases than you would believe, from where you currently stand.

*Often, you can get exactly what you want from the components that are already present in your life. You don't have to go to a whole new place; you just have to chronically define a whole new Vibration.*

The relationship between your *expectation* and *what you're seeing* is the only thing that you ever have the ability to *feel* around. (We just wanted to get that premise established.) Good.

**Questioner:** Okay, thank you.

**Abraham:** Yes, indeed.

### Asheville, North Carolina, Sunday Close

**Abraham:** We have enjoyed this interaction more than words can say. You are Leading Edge creators, and we have gone in places that no one has been before. It is exhilarating to take thought beyond, and it is satisfying to feel the harmony, the aligning, that has taken place with so many of you today.

There has been a theme unfold here that we think is highly productive, and that is a releasing of so many flawed premises and a replacing those flawed premises with these *Law*-based premises. And we would like to leave you with one final one: *We all make too much of all of this. It is simpler than we all make it out to be. Be easy about it. Be kind to yourself. Do things that feel fun. Look for things that bring you relief, and just easily move into that place (your Vortex) where all things that you want have already been lined up for you.*

There is great love here for you. And, as always, we remain blissfully and Eternally incomplete.

# Flawed Premises

1. I am either physical or Non-Physical, either dead or alive.

2. My parents, because they were here long before I was born, and because they are my parents, know better than I do what is right or wrong for me.

3. If I push hard enough against unwanted things, they will go away.

4. I have come here to live the right way of life and to influence others to the same right way of living. . . .

5. Because I am older than you, I am wiser than you; and therefore you should allow me to guide you.

6. Who I am began the day I was born into my physical body. . . .

7. With enough effort, or hard work, I can accomplish anything.

8. To be in harmony with another, we have to want and believe the same things.

9. The path to my joy is through my action. . . .

10. I cannot have everything that I desire, so I have to give up some things that are important to me in order to get others.

11.  If I leave an unwanted situation, I will find what I am looking for.

12.  There is a finite container of resources that we are all dipping into with our requests. . . .

13.  There are right ways and wrong ways to live. . . .

14.  There is a God Who, having considered all things, has come to a final and correct conclusion about everything.

15.  You cannot know, while you are still in your physical body, the true reward or punishment for your physical actions. . . .

16.  By gathering data about the manifestations or results of the way the people of the earth have lived and are living, we can effectively sort them into absolute piles of right and wrong. . . .

17.  Only very special people, like the founder of *our* group, can receive the right message from God. . . .

18.  By ferreting out the undesirable elements in our society, we can eliminate them. . . .

19.  A good relationship is one in which the dominant intention of each person involved is to find agreement and harmony with the other.

20.  When I focus upon things of a physical nature, I am less Spiritual.

21.  It is my job as a parent to have all the answers so that I can teach those answers to my children.

22.  I can criticize successful people and still achieve my own success.

# About the Authors

Excited about the clarity and practicality of the translated information from the Beings who called themselves *Abraham,* **Jerry** and **Esther Hicks** began disclosing their amazing Abraham experience to a handful of close business associates in 1986.

Recognizing the practical results being received by themselves and by those people who were asking meaningful questions regarding the application of the principles of the *Law of Attraction* to finances, bodily conditions, and relationships—and then successfully applying Abraham's answers to their own situations—Jerry and Esther made a deliberate decision to allow Abraham's teachings to become available to an ever-widening circle of seekers of answers to how to live a better life.

Since 1989, using their San Antonio, Texas, conference center as their base, Esther and Jerry have traveled to approximately 50 cities a year (throughout Australia, Canada, England, Ireland, and the United States), presenting a series of interactive *Law of Attraction* Workshops to those leaders who have gathered to participate in this progressive stream of thought. And although worldwide attention has been given to this philosophy of Well-Being by Leading Edge thinkers and teachers who have, in turn, incorporated many of Abraham's concepts into their best-selling books, scripts, lectures, films, and so forth, the primary spread of this material has been from person to person, as individuals begin to discover the value of this form of spiritual practicality in their personal life experiences.

Abraham—a group of obviously evolved Non-Physical teachers—speak their Broader Perspective through Esther. And as they speak to our level of comprehension through a series of loving, allowing, brilliant, yet comprehensively simple essays in print and in sound, they guide us to a clear Connection with our loving, guiding *Inner Being* and to uplifting self-empowerment from our Total Self.

Featuring the concept of the Universal *Law of Attraction,* the Hickses have published more than 800 Abraham-Hicks books, cassettes, CDs, and DVDs (now translated into more than 30 different languages). They may be contacted through their extensive interactive Website at: **www.abraham-hicks.com**; or by mail at Abraham-Hicks Publications, P.O. Box 690070, San Antonio, TX 78269.

Notes

Notes

Notes

# Hay House Titles of Related Interest

*YOU CAN HEAL YOUR LIFE, the movie,*
starring Louise L. Hay & Friends
(available as a 1-DVD program and an expanded 2-DVD set)
Watch the trailer at: **www.LouiseHayMovie.com**

*THE SHIFT, the movie,* starring Dr. Wayne W. Dyer
(available as a 1-DVD program and an expanded 2-DVD set)
Watch the trailer at: **www.DyerMovie.com**

❧

*CREATIVE FLOWDREAMING™: Manifesting Your Dreams
in the Life You've Already Got,* by Summer McStravick

*THE HEART OF LOVE: How to Go Beyond Fantasy to Find
True Relationship Fulfillment,* by Dr. John F. Demartini

*MAXIMIZE YOUR POTENTIAL THROUGH THE
POWER OF YOUR SUBCONSCIOUS MIND FOR AN
ENRICHED LIFE,* by Dr. Joseph Murphy

*SECRETS OF ATTRACTION: The Universal Laws of Love,
Sex, and Romance,* by Sandra Anne Taylor

*SPIRIT-CENTERED RELATIONSHIPS: Experiencing Greater Love
and Harmony Through the Power of Presencing,* by Gay Hendricks,
Ph.D., and Kathlyn Hendricks, Ph.D. (book-with-CD)

*THE WON THING: The "One" Secret to a Totally Fulfilling Life,*
by Peggy McColl

❧

All of the above are available at your local bookstore,
or may be ordered by contacting Hay House (see next page).

❧

We hope you enjoyed this Hay House book. If you'd like to receive our online catalog featuring additional information on Hay House books and products, or if you'd like to find out more about the Hay Foundation, please contact:

Hay House, Inc.
P.O. Box 5100
Carlsbad, CA 92018-5100

**(760) 431-7695 or (800) 654-5126**
**(760) 431-6948 (fax) or (800) 650-5115 (fax)**
**www.hayhouse.com® • www.hayfoundation.org**

*Published and distributed in Australia by:* Hay House Australia Pty. Ltd., 18/36 Ralph St., Alexandria NSW 2015 • *Phone:* 612-9669-4299 • *Fax:* 612-9669-4144 • www.hayhouse.com.au

*Published and distributed in the United Kingdom by:* Hay House UK, Ltd., 292B Kensal Rd., London W10 5BE • *Phone:* 44-20-8962-1230 • *Fax:* 44-20-8962-1239 • www.hayhouse.co.uk

*Published and distributed in the Republic of South Africa by:* Hay House SA (Pty), Ltd., P.O. Box 990, Witkoppen 2068 • *Phone/Fax:* 27-11-467-8904 • info@hayhouse.co.za • www.hayhouse.co.za

*Published in India by:* Hay House Publishers India, Muskaan Complex, Plot No. 3, B-2, Vasant Kunj, New Delhi 110 070 • *Phone:* 91-11-4176-1620 • *Fax:* 91-11-4176-1630 • www.hayhouse.co.in

*Distributed in Canada by:* Raincoast, 9050 Shaughnessy St., Vancouver, B.C. V6P 6E5 • *Phone:* (604) 323-7100 • *Fax:* (604) 323-2600 • www.raincoast.com

## Take Your Soul on a Vacation

Visit **www.HealYourLife.com®** to regroup, recharge, and reconnect with your own magnificence. Featuring blogs, mind-body-spirit news, and life-changing wisdom from Louise Hay and friends.

Visit **www.HealYourLife.com** today!